BREAKING FREE

A troubled young girl's determination to forge a better life

By

Brenda L Gauper

No part of this book may be reproduced, stored in a retrieval system, or transmitted in any form or by any means, electronic, mechanical, photocopying, recording, or otherwise, without the prior written permission of the publisher. Unauthorized use or distribution of this book is strictly prohibited and may result in legal action.

ISBN NO: **979-8-9908632-3-1**

DEDICATION

For every reader who finds a piece of themselves within these chapters, may you find the courage and personal strength to free yourself from anything holding you back from becoming everything that you're meant to be.

May my story be a testament to the power of perseverance and hope.

Table of Contents

PREFACE

Something Is Not Right

I was born in Portland, Oregon. I have one brother, nine years older, and two younger brothers. My father was a home builder, and my mother was a stay-at-home mom.

My father was an extremely hard-working, blue-collar man who was devoted to my mom and to us. He worked six days a week, and his time off was spent in the yard and our little garden, where I learned about the different varieties of cherry tomatoes. Thinking about my father today, what really comes to mind is how selfless he was. He continued to do what was right; he continued to put his obligations and vows before himself. How devastating it would have been for us if he chose otherwise and called it quits. He admitted to me that he had thought of throwing in the towel many times; I guess it was the card he was dealt.

My father developed raw land and built our childhood home on a cul-de-sac, a beautiful split entry with a small octagonal window facing the street, and painted it light pink, my mom's wishes. Our house was located in the beautiful up-and-coming Mt. Tabor neighborhood, and looking east, you could see Mt. Hood. He built many of the homes on this street; it was such a great neighborhood to enjoy my childhood. I had many great memories of the place. We were lucky to live on Mt. Tabor.

In my earliest years, I did not know that anything was wrong or not right. I did not know what I did not have. What child has a clue that all is not well? My mother was physically present, though emotionally unavailable. My father was our stabilizing force, but unfortunately, not powerful enough to circumvent my long, difficult journey, not powerful enough to spare me from what would lie ahead.

It was not until I was 16 that I learned the official diagnosis that my mother was "Manic-Depressive." Until this medical description that actually gave it a name, my brothers and I were always told that she was having a nervous breakdown when she would go into one of her episodes. I have since learned more and more about growing up with a family member who was not well, especially a parent afflicted with mental illness.

One aspect of my childhood, which I have to think was very damaging, was that love was non-existent. I never witnessed my parents expressing any compassion or affection for one another. I never saw the simplest embrace or kiss between them, and definitely never heard the words "I love you" spoken.

I cannot recall a day in my childhood when I received a simple embrace or was told, "I love you." No, not once. Growing up this way had an effect. When my Nanny (Grandma) bent over to give me a little hug, the gesture was so foreign to me. I did not like it. My physical reaction was to stiffen up and pull away from someone who was, in fact, very special to me. As she wrapped her arms around me, I had an adverse reaction.

I did not have any examples of physical closeness. My dad was Norwegian, and Norwegians were known for not being very demonstrative. On weekends, my parents argued in the kitchen while my dad made breakfast. He would chase her away as she ran out…smacking her on the bottom.

When I became older, around the age of 12 or 13, my mother began treating me worse. When I was 12 years old, I went strawberry picking to earn some money. When I arrived home from a long, tiring day, I came in through the front door, filthy-dirty and sweaty. She was standing at the top of the stairs, raging mad, demanding to know where I was. When I told her that I was out strawberry picking, she started losing it.

She immediately began accusing me of lying, and of being out with boys instead of strawberry picking. I was crying and denying it. As she kept on, to prove my innocence, I reached into the pocket of my jeans and started pulling out dirty, strawberry-stained dollar bills, one after the other, throwing them down on the floor, desperately trying to help her see the truth.

None of this convinced her. She smacked me across the face and pulled me into the bathroom just down the hall to wash my mouth out with soap.

She yelled at all of us constantly, ordering us out of the house so she could take a nap. She demanded the lights to be off!

"None of you kids are ever going to college. We can't afford it!" I was fairly young, much too young to even contemplate higher education, the first time my mother barked out that statement. It was as though this and other future dreams had to be nipped in the bud right away, just in case. "Don't you ever expect a big wedding from us," she would tell me, thereby dashing a future dream before it was even thought up.

As an adult today, I have no ill will toward her. In fact, I have empathy and compassion for what she must have gone through. I can't imagine living with the level of depression she had. I know she suffered.

Unfortunately, for me, there would be some fallout. An unhealthy launch. My childhood created many bad behavior's - like looking for love and comfort in all the wrong places – and escaping with alcohol - habits that took decades to overcome.

CHAPTER ONE

Worst Chapter with a Blessing

It was almost the end of my freshman year, and school would be letting out in a few more weeks. I left school for the day - a day like any other - and started hitchhiking home from Marshall High School. I lived a few miles up the way on Mt. Tabor, and this was the most economical form of commuting. This way, I could pocket the bus money.

Standing with my thumb out on SE 82nd Ave, it would never take long, usually just minutes, before a ride would pull over for me. I was always picked up by men and had gotten myself into several dangerous close calls; many were not pulling over to be the "nice guy."

I was a very naive 14-year-old, only five ft one and about 110 pounds. I had blonde hair and blue eyes, making myself

11

available and vulnerable to a world of potential predators. Once again, my method of transportation proved reliable. A very dark-complexioned man pulled over along the shoulder of the road, waiting for me to approach the car, and without a care in the world, I quickly made a beeline to the long gold four-door car waiting and got in.

This happen chance moment would change the course and future of my entire life.

I was picked up by Ray Hernandez, a much older Mexican man with very thick, wavy black hair down to his shoulder. He had dark brown eyes, and the whites of his eyes were slightly yellowish. His skin was rugged, with a couple of facial scars, a dark mustache, and a goatee. He was wearing blue jeans and a black tee shirt with a pack of cigarettes in the pocket.

His amateur tattoo showed at the bicep, and it said "Ray" in very simple cursive. It looked as if he could have done it himself. He seemed normal enough. No bells were going off telling me that I needed to get out of the car. As he was driving me toward home up the four-lane highway, he was telling me about his auto detailing shop that he was heading to and asked if I was interested in a job. It entailed detailing cars, and I could start that afternoon. I was all for it and agreed. I was thrilled.

This was my lucky day! I really wanted a job, and I had been struggling to make that happen, as I loathed the idea of working at a fast-food joint. I wanted to do anything other than that. This was perfect.

I was a hard worker and loved to clean! (Such a crazy thing to love, but it's true.) This type of work couldn't have been more fitting for me. Ray did work for all of the used car dealerships up and down SE 82nd Ave. I had been handpicked. We drove out several miles into Gresham and arrived at a large commercial building located on 181st near I-84. The building stood alone, with nothing but undeveloped land around it and a boarded-up house. The only other sign of civilization was a Chevron gas station just north toward the Banfield freeway. We were in the boonies, but that did not concern me. Getting a job was all that mattered, and wherever I was, it was irrelevant.

We got started right away, and he showed me the ropes. Demonstrating, he gave me instruction on all the steps to detail a car from bumper to bumper. After filling a bucket with warm, sudsy water and using a long bristle brush, you started on the dash, slopping the soapy water over everything, including the seats and floors. The soap suds would turn a muddy brown, especially on the carpets, but disappear with the shop vac.

Basically, all the cars that came through his shop were old beaters and would be transformed by the complete detail.

I was so excited to earn some money. My last job was while I was in the 8th grade, working at Eastgate Movie Theater, selling movie tickets and popcorn for $1.95 per hour. The two previous summers, I picked strawberries and raspberries and delivered a local newspaper called "The Press" on Wednesdays. Ray offered to pay me $5.00 per car. I felt I'd hit the jackpot. I guess I really didn't think it through; a complete detail would take two to three hours, including cleaning the trunk, windows inside and out, along with tires and wheels. Having the opportunity to finally make some money was what mattered.

My focus was on the five dollars, and I wanted to complete as many cars as I could.

Ray picked me up after school from that day forward. Taking the job was a dramatic change for me. I stepped out of one life and stepped completely into another. High school was over, as I once knew it. My freshman boyfriend and my peers with whom I'd socialized and partied with came to an end. I was fine with that; I really did not have any strong connections or circumstances that kept me from giving up my teenage life.

He showed up every day, no longer on 82nd but at the doors of my school, parked and waiting for me. He would drive me directly to the shop to start work. After detailing a couple of cars, he would buy beer and groom me to be his girlfriend. Hanging out at the shop and drinking beer was not anything foreign to me. It was not any different from what I would be doing with my group of high school friends after school anyway. I was, however, not with high school friends. I had stepped into an adult world that I was way too young for. I was being pursued by a much older man. I would learn that Ray was 12 years older than I was and married with three young boys. He had left his wife, and she was on welfare while he preyed on young girls. He named another girl from Marshall that he had hired, and I knew her. Her name was "Stormy." I suspected she was another troubled gal.

My not going home after school was neither here nor there. It just did not matter. My mother was not at home and had not been home my entire freshman year. She was institutionalized at Dammasch State Mental Hospital in Salem, Oregon, and my dad worked long days. I knew I would not be missed.

This breakdown was one of my mom's worst; She had been admitted right before my freshman year began. My mom

15

was about 5 feet 7 inches tall, usually about 140 lbs. and was now down to 95 lbs. She had deep, dark circles under her eyes and stood in the corners of the room staring at you, almost as though she was afraid of you. She seemed paranoid. She never answered the phone, and she did not speak. I would see her holding a small plate and eating the leftover crusts from the peanut butter and jelly sandwiches left by my brothers. We all just seemed to carry on around her. I suppose we just kind of ignored her. On another occasion, I witnessed her sitting on the floor in her bedroom with her head staring straight up at the ceiling. She did not move. She seemed literally frozen in place with her eyes locked onto the ceiling.

I believe she had been kept home way too long this time and needed to go to the hospital months earlier. Her mother (my grandma) insisted that all she needed was good nutrition. My grandma did not believe in medication or medical doctors, so my dad surrendered to the pressure and let her be. My grandmother and my aunt had spent some time at our house that summer, trying to help, but unfortunately, my mom only got worse and worse. I believe had she stayed home much longer, she would have died. These breakdowns always began exactly the same way, in a full manic phase and a complete high!

She would be bouncing off the walls with boundless energy, in a fantastic mood, staying up all night with the cupboards open, pots and pans clanging, and all the lights on. She had laundry going, Christian radio on in the kitchen, music in the bathroom, and the TV on in the living room and was twirling round and round, singing, "I'm a poet and doesn't know it" over and over. She was full of enthusiasm, pounding her hips, saying, "Mark my words, I'm going to get rid of these pounds!" She expressed grandiose plans and was very euphoric for several days. And then, without sleeping, eating, or resting for days, she would CRASH! At this point the party was over, just like that. The lights were off, and the music died.

Finally, she was admitted. This was not the typical week or two stay in a traditional hospital. This would be a much slower go as she would remain there for an entire year. My father would have us go visit her on the weekends, taking me and my two younger brothers on the long drive to Salem. We had to go, and I dreaded it. I was completely void of any feelings for her. I know this sounds horrible to say, but there was nothing there.

Week after week, during our visits with my mother, without fail, she would start in on one of her tangents. Trying to get my dad's attention to the matter, smacking him on the shoulder and telling him that I was pregnant. She was absolutely convinced that I was pregnant, pleading, "Al, do something. Brenda is pregnant." She was so persistent with her accusations that, after weeks of hearing this, it started really scaring me. Could this somehow be true? This can't be! I admit. I did not have regular periods, but I had never had sex, either! It was all so nuts.

I loved that she was gone. I loved that my mother was not at home. I quickly took on all of the home tasks, cleaning, vacuuming, and even mowing the lawn. My dad and I went grocery shopping on the weekend with my list for the week ahead. Eventually, he would let me buy a six-pack of beer that I could take to my boyfriend's house. I can't blame him. I was able to manipulate the situation... getting the beer in the cart. I know that he meant no harm, but I think now that fourteen was pretty young. I prepared meals, school lunches...and made cookies for Christmas. I did laundry and looked after my two younger brothers. I'm not sure what that really looked like, but I did a pretty good job. I continued this role throughout the year; I felt that I was a huge help to my father.

Breaking Free

I took advantage of my mother not being at home. I had total freedom. I skipped school, smoked pot, and had many high-school partiers come over during the school day. We were not quite the stoners who would hang out on the corner and smoke pot in front of the high school; we were a step up. We lived on Mt. Tabor! The rich hippies. We would drink beer and crank up the stereo, playing Jethro Tull, the Allman Brothers, and Charlie Daniels…country rock of all kinds. My best friend and I were experimenting with cross-tops (speed) as we wanted to be thin. We would each stand side by side and compare how flat we could get our stomachs. While high on speed, I would scurry from room to room throughout the house and clean like a crazy person. I loved it. Cleaning, to me, has always been fun. Possibly, it was a form of adding order to my life, something that I was in control of. Visually, everything had to be perfect. When I was younger, I had a very shaggy rug in my bedroom and hated to see any footprints on it; I would tell my neighbor friends that we were going to play a game…no one could step on the rug. I think they thought it was fun for a minute, but as soon as they decided it was not and started stepping on the rug again, I would immediately take my hand behind them and fluff up the spots where they stepped. Maybe all of this fanaticism was part of my DNA?

My best friend and I were both freshmen, and our peers were pretty much all guys… mostly juniors and seniors. In my mind, having a sophomore boyfriend and being included in the group somehow made me way cooler than the cheerleaders. No one played football or went to the games; we never attended the assemblies. That was always the perfect opportunity to head up to the top of Tabor to smoke pot. The Mt. Tabor boys picked me up every morning and gave me a ride to school, never without passing the joint. I hated it when I could not remember my locker combination. Standing there as the bell rang to be in the classroom, panic was setting in. The tardy bell would ring in five minutes. I looked up and down the hallway as the last kid cleared out, and I was still standing there, waiting for the fog to clear. *What the hell is my locker number?* I recall the worry, *what if I have to go to the office to ask them what it is?* I just stood there until it came to me.

Throughout the year, Dammasch would let my mother out on passes to come home for a few days, then would return back. By now, we were all getting along without her and growing up way too fast. The guidance that I'm sure I needed would not be my story. Things were as they were. We were all free-range growing up, and each was affected in different ways by my mom's disability. For much of our lives, her condition took center stage, leaving us to fend for ourselves. I truly believe that becoming independent is of utmost importance, but too much independence can be damaging. Unfortunately, we do not know what we do not know. I had no awareness or alarm bells sounding that I was heading in the wrong direction. There was no one to catch it. My mother was unavailable, and my dad was doing everything possible to keep a roof over our heads. He had a full plate, where I was...was not on anyone's radar. He had mentioned to me that he had thought about throwing in the towel. That was a surprise confession, but he never did. He definitely remained true to his vows, for better or worse. I believe my dad had to look to the State for help with her financially...all of the hospitalizations were becoming unaffordable.

So, jumping ahead, this first year of high-school was coming to a close, and summer break began. Ray would round the cul-de-sac and pick me up at my home every morning. I would work all day detailing cars, to drinking beer, and falling deeper into the life of an abused girl. We were having sex (unwanted, intoxicated). Then, he would take me home every night after sunset and repeat the next day. I was with him every day except Sunday. This was my life…I worked and spent all of my time at the shop. Some afternoons, we would knock off early and drive to the river (to drink, of course) or take a break, where he would teach me to drive. I loved that he would buy me a meal, a big burger or something. I guess I started feeling looked after. On occasion, we would go to a restaurant called the Satellite on 181st in Gresham. I had not yet experienced looking over a menu. This was a big deal for me. Going into a restaurant was new. We would sit side by side, and he would always choose a booth where I could not gaze out around the room to see any patrons. He chose a corner end booth so that I would face a wall. I never thought much of it at the time, but it was a definite warning sign.

It was the summer of 1975. My mother was back home from Dammasch State Mental Hospital, and I would turn 15 years old in July. I definitely was not happy that she was back. She treated me poorly, and I wanted to avoid her. Having her at home only reinforced my wanting to be gone all day. Every morning, I would watch for Ray to drive into the cul-de-sac and run out of the house to go to work, never giving off a clue that I was (by now) involved with a man 12 years older than me.

I believe my father was having financial difficulty by now. With the expensive property taxes living on Mt. Tabor and all of my mom's hospital bills mounting, we could no longer remain living in my childhood home. This caused us to pack up and move to a much smaller, modest Cape Cod home in the old Hollywood neighborhood of Portland. With all that my dad had to deal with and so much focus on my mom, it took the attention off me. This, of course, made it all so much easier for Ray to tighten his grip and continue on in his mission, putting his plan into action day in and day out.

My dad was able to purchase the home we moved into with the furniture included. I was so thrilled to receive a beautiful antique bedroom set for my new room, located at ground level, with a small window leading out to the backyard. I helped in the move from Mt. Tabor to 49th and Halsey and continued working for Ray.

I don't recall why things got set up the way they did as to how Ray would pay me. I'm sure that it was Ray's idea not to give me regular pay. He had me keep track of all my car details on a paper worksheet in the shop office. He said that he would pay me at the end of the summer. I really did not need any money paid to me on a regular basis. I would have just saved it anyway, and I agreed to the terms. When it was finally payday, he handed me three one-hundred-dollar bills…at 5 dollars per car, this would be my pay for completing 60 full details. It was a big day for me! The excitement to cash in after more than two months of keeping tally. I put the three hundred-dollar bills in my pocket, and he got the beer. He kept me out way too late that night and would not take me home. We stayed at an apartment belonging to people he knew. By morning, it was time to take me home. On top of my worry as to what to say to my parents when I arrived home, I dug into my pocket and panicked; my money was gone!! I was heartbroken. Ray acted concerned and helped look around for the money, searching his car, in and under the seats…everywhere. Nothing. I returned home and told my parents that all of my money was missing and that I had lost it. My parents both told me that Ray had stolen it from me. I refused to believe this.

By the end of the summer, it was time to think about going back to school. I was now 15 years old and going to start my sophomore year back at Marshall High. I started feeling that I was in a bad place. This life was making no sense. I had no interaction with anyone my age, and I had zero contact with a single high school friend or neighborhood friend, for that matter. I think I was waking up and knew that I had to get back to my peers. Feeling some embarrassment and shame about my choices, I decided that I wanted to put all of this into the rear-view mirror.

So, I did it. I broke things off and returned immediately to the high-school life that I had left behind. Trying to resume and re-connect where I had left off, going back to week-end keggers, seeing all the people from my previous year, and wanting so desperately to belong. All was the same, and nothing had changed really. Then, after only a couple of months, I started thinking everything had changed, quickly realizing that I was no better off. I no longer had the cool boyfriend from the year before, the most popular party boy. His parents owned a bar, and he could supply all of the taps to the kegs. He knew where all the parties were, and I was his girlfriend. The entire Freshman year had been weekend parties along with my very best girlfriend from 6th grade. We were a duo! Now, as I attempted to restore and re-create my previous high school life, I found myself sitting at a weekend party, looking around the room and feeling completely alone. I no longer felt any sense of belonging; I had no bonds, and I felt like an outsider. I can still visualize this time in my life. What was I ever going to do? How was I ever going to take care of myself? I had no real interests and was not applying myself in school. I had no direction, guidance, or confidence. I also felt very uncomfortable around adults. I felt that they were against me. Somehow, I feared them. I believed, they believed, that I was a bad person. How could anyone see any good in me? As my own mother thought I was despicable. I recall feeling very lost and very worried about my future.

Then, shazam… right at that time: There was Ray! He picked me up hitch hiking again on my way home from school, admitting that he was always on the lookout for me. I got in, he pulled me close, gave me a big hug, and offered for me to come to the shop. I was back!! This was it, what I chose! I lacked self-worth, and I certainly did not have a plan B. I had no idea that there were bad people out there. I was prepared for nothing. I wasn't close to anyone, and for those reasons, I was especially vulnerable to the likes of Ray. Being someone with no real ideas or opinions of right or wrong or knowledge of good or bad made me ripe for the picking.

Breaking Free

From that fall of my sophomore year, I became much more involved with him and gave into the idea that I was his girlfriend. It was not that he was my boyfriend. It was more like a surrender. I gave in to an arrangement. Providing me with employment was enough to seal the deal. I definitely did not fall for him. I have not a single recollection of caring for him in any way. My awareness that something was not right with this picture was void; I had no concept of how wrong this all was and had no expectations for myself. None of this mattered. I just wanted to work and believed that I was being taken care of in some way. I suppose he was my new provider. This all was fine with me, especially as I had no interest in ever being home.

For the rest of my sophomore year, I would hitch-hike to school every morning…or take a bus, whichever came first…the bus or a ride. One morning, I quickly put my thumb out as I recognized a car with blacked-out windows. I had seen this car previously. He pulled over, and I got in, sat down, and closed the door. As I looked to my left at his lap, I noticed he had a gun pointed at me. He was holding it with his left hand down low, stabilized across his lap. He said, "Don't try anything and you won't get hurt."

I looked at the gun as he was holding it and thought for a second that it was not real. I immediately replied, "Don't YOU try anything!" I said this back to him in a much more commanding way than his command to me. I recall being mad that he was doing this. It definitely helped to cover my fear and uncertainty. He made a fast, hard left down a side street and started picking up speed, and I started making my plan. I swung my door open and pushed using all my strength and started shifting sideways to swing my legs out; I was going to jump out at any cost. This must have really spooked him as he then came to an immediate stop. I stepped out, slammed the door, and returned home. I was very mad, told my mom about this and we contacted the police. When they came to take the report, they told me that this individual had picked up two girls just two days prior, used the same gun… and drove them over to Marine Drive, where they were both sexually violated. I don't know what came over me, how I took charge and did not panic or experience any real fear. Tragically, they were not so lucky.

After telling Ray all about it, he drove around looking for this car. He was acting pretty mad and did have a very bad temper. It also seemed like something to do: just pound down the beers and drive around; all pretty stupid! A day or so later,

I was contacted by the police, who said that they had apprehended the creep. They found the car and found him living at a trailer park. I was not needed to testify, as what they had on him by the two previous victims was enough.

I continued getting myself to school by bus or an anonymous ride. I had to travel about 10 miles and wanted to make it as efficient as possible, either method was fine. On a couple of occasions, I pretended not to notice as they masturbated. I knew what was going on and never looked. I just sat there in disgust, saying to myself, *"Please just get me to where I'm going."* On one occasion, I did ask the guy to let me out, and he replied, "Not until I'm done" What shitty, gross people there are!

Making my choice to return to the shop was a complete diversion from staying a high schooler, closing the door on where I was probably to be. I had completely abandoned my peers and was a true loner, except for Ray. It was almost as though I had succumbed to a spell that had been put on me. Some kind of power pulled me away. I found that I looked forward to getting picked up and taken to the shop, especially getting something to eat. That was a highlight for me. I worked every day after school, and as unhealthy as my circumstances were, I think settling into a routine added some structure to my life. Obviously, I was searching for something. I just wanted to belong.

The long, dreary days of my daily life slowly changed from fall to winter. For Christmas, Ray bought me an 8-track player that I opened in the living room with my family. My brothers and I set it up in my bedroom and gathered together just hanging out. This, I felt then, was where I belonged! Home, like any 15-year-old. I was not to be pulled away from my family, my life, or my future by this perpetuator. How could he feel the least bit good about being involved with such a young, naive, and gullible girl?

As I think back, and visualize myself in the living room at Christmas, with my dad in his easy chair next to the table-top tree and all of my brothers sitting around the room, the trays of cold cuts, potato salad, and my mom's relishes, it is bitter-sweet. The sense of family that holiday was still a comfort for me, though I could feel my life-changing. My involvement with Ray was taking hold, and there would be no turning back. I was moving on; I had already been captured.

Emotional turmoil-early Spring

Breaking Free

One afternoon, after being smacked upside the head a few times by Ray, he dropped me off back at home. The abuse at this point in the relationship was just beginning, just an out-of-the-blue episode at this point. As I got to the house and entered through the back door, I was experiencing some kind of an emotional breakdown. I was crying uncontrollably and could not catch my breath. I was desperate for some kind of emotional comfort and started searching for my parents and actually calling out for my mom as I scurried from one room to another, frantically trying to find someone. I darted around, gasping for air as my heavy tears covered my face. I could find no one. No one was home. No one would hear my cries reaching out.

This was my first time being this upset, experiencing such desperation, my first sense of wanting help, some kind of rescue, someone to help make everything OK. I wanted to tell someone what was happening and desperately wanted someone to be there. The house was still, and I would suffer alone.

I have no idea what would have happened if either of my parents had been home. Would their being there have altered my course, pulled me off the path that I would inevitably go down? I somehow believe that it would have, that I would have outed him. As I calmed down in all the silence, I never sought out any further rescue. I tucked it all away, hid the tears, and buried the shame of it all. I was in severe trouble; my life was in the hands of a monster, and I did not have the maturity or the wisdom to see things clearly. I pulled myself together and did not give off a clue that I was in a really bad place. That afternoon was the only moment that I cried out for my mom, the one and only time. And she wasn't home. This brief window of correcting my course closed as fast as it opened. I still lived at home; time was running out.

Ray was trying to get me to run away from home, to join him and leave my life. As he was coercing me in this direction, I was beginning to overhear my parents' conversations taking place. I would stand at the top of the stairs and listen to them in the finished basement area while they were watching TV. They were talking about Ray. They were discussing getting him for statuary rape; they knew what was up. It had to be obvious to them my involvement with him. At times, I would sneak out of my bedroom window after Ray would drop me off just so I could stay out a little longer. The window was an old double-hung wood frame that I could slide up and slip out of into the back yard. It was the worst shock, when I returned, and the bedroom window was locked. I would have to come in from the side door leading into the kitchen, where they could bust me. The violation was always handled, with them both yelling at me. Growing up and being yelled at was the norm, and this way of trying to get our attention was all they knew. It was the only tool in the toolbox. I don't recall specific threats from them. None were verbalized, but I knew I did not want them to ever act on getting Ray in trouble. Hearing them talk about this was alarming for me. At one point, I took off from home for a week or two, and they contacted the shop and wanted me to come home. They never took any steps or legal action against him. It was too late; I was too far out of the gate by now. I would have run away and resented them. I belonged to my captor.

Ray actually lived at the shop. He used the office space to bed down at night on a futon after leaving his wife sometime earlier. This was also where we spent much of our time, the only place to escape, to get out of the elements and take refuge from the cold. Heated with a space heater, we dashed in to warm up after working in the shop while the winter months rolled on. The room was small, but there was a large desk where I could set up, and prepare a meal in my electric skillet. Even if the shop was too cold to work in, I would spend the entire day with him regardless…six days a week. As spring began, we could get more jobs done. I went with him to deliver the detailed cars back to the dealerships and pick up our next jobs. The word was out…Ray had the best interior detail shop going. Thanks to me, of course. He also did auto-body work and painted cars, all of which he'd learned in prison. He was born in Colorado, and he and his sister were both abandoned by their parents. Both were still babies. One set of grandparents took him, and the other set took his sister. They lived in separate towns, and he grew up dirt poor. He would never meet her.

He also explained to me that the reason that he never had any cavities was that he never had any sweets growing up and that he would eat toothpaste for a treat. He only made it to the 6th grade in school, then started stealing cars, joined a gang, and was in and out of jail. He told me that he was always breaking out of jail, and they could not keep him in custody. So, by the age of 16 years old, the justice system made an exception and placed him in a state penitentiary where you were to be at least 18 years old. He told me this story with pride, saying that he was the youngest person ever allowed; they made an exception for him. It was like a notch on his belt; it was somehow cool that he was the youngest one in prison. We all want to be proud of something, and this was his badge.

It was around late May or so, and the days were still very cool, but they stayed light longer. One day, standing in the office area of the shop, I looked down and noticed a poof in my lower belly. As I stared down at this unfamiliar bulge… I tried to see if I could suck it in and make it go away? Rather bewildered, I started joking and said to Ray, "Maybe I'm pregnant," not believing it for a second. I was only kidding. He had always told me that he could never get me pregnant. Within another minute, I heard my words come back to me. What had I just said? The rush of those words hit me. Oh my gosh. What if I was? Holy shit!

The joke quickly changed into a potential reality, all within a matter of minutes. From that moment on, I could not get this possibility off my mind. The whole idea grew on me. I could not think about anything else. I started visualizing having my own little person, someone with whom to love and share life.

Each day, this was getting more real in my head. I had to get checked out. This was not a passing moment. This probable reality lay squarely on my lap. So much to process, especially knowing what awful circumstances I was in. I made an appointment for a pregnancy test at a Multnomah County building on 122nd and Glisan. Ray drove me and stayed in the car. It wasn't as though I was in a lovey-dovey relationship where I wanted to share such important moments. While I waited for the results, I paced the large room back and forth…very excited and very nervous all at the same time. I could not sit down for a minute, pacing, crossing my fingers, hoping and praying that the results were going to come back positive. I did not want to hear anything else! They finally came out to the waiting area to give me the results that I desperately wanted; it was positive; I was pregnant. All the worry and concern of this not being the case fell away. I felt such relief. This is exactly what I was hoping for!

Ray was waiting for me in the car, and he made sure not to come in. (I can see why now, as he was wanted for child support for all three of his boys. A true deadbeat!) Before I left the building to find him out in the parking lot and tell him my good news, I used the outgoing phone on the wall to make a call to Planned Parenthood to schedule my first pre-natal exam. I informed them that I had just got my results from a pregnancy test and that I was pregnant. They did not ask any questions and scheduled me one month out for my first appointment. I'm not sure why I was scheduled so far out. I imagine most people are just a couple of months along, and therefore, they probably assumed a more common scenario. This ended up not being the case.

I showed up at Planned Parenthood on SE Belmont for my first pre-natal appointment, excited to get some care started. The woman who saw me spent the first two hours of our time together trying to talk me into an abortion. She would not stop. She was relentless. I just sat there as she went on and on. I let her know that I wanted and planned to keep my baby and was not the least bit interested in what SHE wanted me to do. Clearly, she had HER opinion. I sat there as long as it took. I was very calm and unshakable. I knew what I was doing. The entire two hours seemed more and more like sitting in an interrogation room than being seen for family planning! As she tried to wear me down, I remained unwavering. FINALLY, when she realized that I was not going to consider it and there was nothing she could say or do to change my mind, she started talking to me about adoption. Another waste of time. I was not interested in that either. I was feeling a real sense of someone trying to overpower me, and I had to remain strong, though there was no chance that I wouldn't. I viewed her more like another adult with power and authority, someone who was not on my side. I'm sure she was very frustrated with me as she was getting nowhere. She finally said, "OK, let's proceed with the exam."

She asked me how far along I was, and I told her I had no idea; I could not help with this answer at all. Since I did not have regular periods to begin with, I had no clue! I did not even know when I had had my last period. I never kept track of things like that. I guess I could have told her that I was losing my hair and that my gums had been bleeding for the last several months, but that was actually hindsight to these questions.

Finally, the exam started, and she said that she was going to measure me from the top of my belly down. She placed a skinny cloth tape measure at the top of my belly just under the breast area, ran it down to the very bottom of my tummy bulge, and said, "Oh! Well, you are 5 ½ months pregnant! You are past the abortion stage." Unbelievable! What the hell, what a screwed-up facility. Had she only begun with the exam from the beginning, she would not have wasted both of our time.

By this time, it was already July, school had let out, and I was very pregnant. So far, so good. I was pulling it off. My

Muslin smocks were giving me the cover I needed. After getting the news as to how far along I was and then getting a due date at the end of October, I remember being really glad that I was as far along as I was. I just couldn't believe that I only had about 3 more months to go to the beginning of my new life. I had only told one person, my very best friend Tammie, that I was pregnant. I caught up with her in the stairwell at Marshall High and told her my news just before school let out. She said, "What are you going to do?" I told her that I was going to keep the baby. I know she did not approve, but we still remained best friends.

I was doing everything possible to hide my growing stomach from my parents. I looped a rubber band over the brass button on my jeans and looped it through the button hole to customize. Fortunately, it was 1975. Loose-fitting muslin smocks with embroidered necklines were very much in fashion. What luck! I was trying to hide my pregnancy as long as I could. I knew enough to know that this was not going to be glorious news for my parents, and the clock was ticking on how much longer I could keep this hidden. With my 16th birthday coming up on July 28th, I set it as some kind of a goal…to make it to that date before I ever got found out. I figured it was going to be much easier to let my parents know if I was 16 yrs. old instead of 15 yrs. old. Well, it didn't happen that way.

I spent every waking hour away from home during the week, but I did stay home on Sundays. I thought it was the right thing to do, at least be home one day a week. One day to not work, a day for laundry, and a day to give my home life at least that much consideration.

This Sunday became memorable... I was helping my mom and dad in the kitchen peeling potatoes, my mom to the left of me near the sink, and my dad to the right at the stove. It was a very small kitchen, and the three of us were all in there together, only feet apart. My father was very much a meat and potatoes man and made nice dinners on the weekends, a tradition. While I was standing at the pull-out cutting board working on the potatoes, out of nowhere...I didn't see it coming. My mom grabbed my muslin smock, yanked it up, and yelled, "Are you pregnant?"

It was all so fast and startling I tried desperately to suck my stomach in as hard as I could and just replied, "No, I've just been eating a little too much lately." I had no idea what to say or what to do. From that second, I knew that I was busted. She was frantic and started yelling at my dad in a very harsh tone to convince him what was going on. He just continued cooking at the stove. He did not respond. Nothing more was said. I wondered what was going through his mind.

I knew the gig was up. The cat was out of the bag. I went to the phone that evening to call Ray and let him know that my parents knew that I was pregnant and that he was going to have to come over and tell them that it was true. The next evening, Ray came over. The four of us were seated at the dining room table when Ray spoke up. He let them know that it was true. I was pregnant, and I was going to keep the baby. He said that he was going to take very good care of us. While talking to them, he made a promise that we would never be on welfare, trying to assure them that everything was going to be OK. He seemed very convincing. I felt in good hands listening to him and believed what he was saying. It was so nice to hear someone saying how things were going to be. It gave me comfort and less worry about where things were headed.

It's all so odd to think about this now. None of this was good news - the happy announcement that a daughter would bring to her parents, that she was in love, and they were planning their "happily ever after." This was not one of those stories. This was so far from that. I just wanted to have my baby, and he was my ticket. I saw it no other way. I did not have any warm feelings or affection for him. This was not a big deal, though, as I had never experienced those emotions for anyone. Fortunately, how I felt about Ray was irrelevant to my objective, having my baby. After he was done speaking, my dad stood up from the table, turned toward the kitchen, and left the room. He did not say a single word. To this day, I have to wonder what the heck was going through his mind. Ray left, and the days resumed as they had.

The realization of being pregnant took the front stage. I started eating better, taking my multivitamins and loved the fact that I no longer had to hold in my stomach. It was something that I trained myself to do, and I held my tummy in to where it became second nature. I could fully relax my belly and did not have to hide my pregnancy any longer. Ray bought me one maternity top and one pair of pants. I wore this outfit every day. Finally, some official clothes without a rubber band holding my jeans up.

Not long after Ray confirmed the reality of my circumstances at the table that evening in July, my mom had another nervous breakdown and went right back to Dammasch. This news was all too much for her. I learned with bi-polar, people cannot handle the ups and downs in life. It could be anything, from a very sad event to the happiest of events.

By now, fall was approaching, and I was due at the end of October. My mom was out of the house, and there would be no going back to high school to start my junior year. Those days were over. I was free. I believed that my new life ahead was all on track. I was going to have a baby; I was going to have someone to love and someone to love me. I had many visions of a little girl. I would visualize myself driving up to park alongside my parent's house, and she would jump out of the car with medium dark curly bouncy hair and run inside. All of my thoughts and visions never included Ray. I just saw myself, only her and me. He was never in the picture.

Ray set us up in a shady old motel out on Sandy Blvd. This area of Portland was very seedy and low-budget, located on an unkempt highway without any sidewalks. It was a week-to-week rental, a single-story stucco building called the Royal Rose Motel, with one-bedroom units and kitchenettes. It was dreary and dimly lit inside with dark wood paneling and yellow-tinged roller shades to draw down, along with mismatched furniture that looked like it came from Goodwill.

There was a front door facing into a courtyard, with a back door and a covered area where you could park.

Ray knew that I was his now. Now that I was fully out of my parents' house, he had acquired full ownership. The circumstances before me would be my new life, and I willingly surrendered. Nothing was close to being normal or healthy in this relationship, but I hadn't a clue. What was normal? How perfect for Ray. I was a clean slate, void of any data. I had not been pre-programmed; I didn't get the needed input growing up to have any *expectations*. Without these examples of "normal" loving relationships, I would have been perfect for him. I was submissive, made no demands, and asked for nothing. We were not some regular couple, starting out... discussing all of our future plans! I was not someone who had it together. My sense of self was very effed up. I was a lost, screwed-up kid and, therefore, easily sucked into this situation. I was not ready to be in this place with this man. I was still a child. My sense of Ray was more of a caretaker. He was my provider and my ticket to being able to keep my baby. He was the only way that I was going to pull this off. It was a package deal.

Breaking Free

This is when the abuse really started ramping up, and all of his training could really begin. He had full control, and I was his unsuspecting victim. He targeted a young one, someone without her own identity, someone without any awareness or concern that things were not quite right, someone who would not give him any trouble, someone so damaged and broken she was unable to see the hell she was in. I had no ability to see the horror ahead of me. I was someone he could fully train to comply and obey. I had no previous instruction that could get in his way. I was completely malleable, someone who could be programmed on how to act.

I'm not sure why Ray was forthcoming with this. I would think that he would have wanted to keep this all to himself, but he made a big admission. He told me that he always knew that he could get me pregnant, and that was going to be his way of having me one day. Hearing his admission fell on deaf ears. I heard what he said, though I felt no reaction either way. By now, so much had changed. Now that I was pregnant and actually OK with it, I didn't understand why the confession. Maybe he wanted to get something off of his chest? To think that all the while, he had been plotting out some kind of a union, a way of having me? I think it kind of says everything right there: I would become his prey. I had no awareness as to how I was going to be acquired by him. I suppose his plan made some sense in some way. He must have known that there would be no other way of having me. If I hadn't become pregnant, I'm sure I would have gotten away.

Ray drank every day. On warm summer days, he had me drinking beers along with him, but the minute that I felt the slightest buzz, I did not take another drink. I was thinking of my baby. I could not believe what was ahead as I looked down on my growing belly. I felt that I had been transplanted into that moment. The speed of my life changing so quickly was so dramatic. The thoughts of just being in high school, standing in the crowded doorway looking out for Ray's car, and now sitting on the lawn with my legs stretched out before me. I begin fully embracing my new reality. The visions of my old life faded. I soaked in the sunrays on my face and felt at peace.

It was near the end of my pregnancy when the real physical violence started. While in some kind of a rage, he shoved me back into a wall. We were in the shop office, and with both hands, he grabbed the neck of my shirt and tore it apart. This was the beginning of endless beatings. None were ever provoked. I just became smaller and smaller as his complete control took over.

With his newly acquired ownership of my life, Ray could start laying down the rules and close the walls around his human chattel. At the motel, the yellowed, nicotine-stained blinds were always to be pulled down. It didn't matter if it was a beautiful, clear, sunny day. There was always a depressing, yellowish tone in the room. I was not allowed to have them open for a little natural daylight or to see the light of day outside. I did not see these signs as red flags at the time, that he was an insecure madman. I think I just complied; I was mute. The more and more control they have over you, the worse and worse it gets! It's all so psychotic. The effects of having no voice, or complete fear of ever developing one, causes one to be taken more and more advantage of.

My due date was fast approaching, and I detailed cars for as long as I could. I was young and physically fit and only gained about 16 pounds during my pregnancy. Being at the shop was pretty much my life, and I had no connections with anyone else. I also felt that I did not want anyone to witness my involvement with Ray. I still had a sense of embarrassment about my involvement with him. He was much older, and we did not have a thing in common. Talk about a mismatch. He was very much a hard-ass with nothing going for him. He also had an air of scariness to him, someone you could see in a gang. I wouldn't have wanted any of my friends or even my family to observe my environment. I very much lived in a well-constructed form of isolation.

At the time, I just lived my life one day at a time and did not think deeply or ponder on "how the hell did I get here"? This entire road was worth it to have my baby. Fall was closing in, and it was now late October. The last few weeks, I just waited it out in the skanky motel until I went into labor. I spent my days alone.

My labor began fairly late into the evening on November 7th. As the contractions started, I rolled myself side to side until they passed. It was time to get to the hospital. I was only a couple of centimeters when we arrived and had to walk the halls for hours before I could have a room. It was a very long and tiring night for me. The doctors had to give me something to slow the contractions down so I could get a little sleep between them. Each one woke me up. I was so exhausted that I would fall right back to sleep until the next one. By morning, it was go time. My contractions were coming closer and closer together, and I was really struggling. I wanted them to give me anything to get me through. I felt like dying.

By morning, at 9:38 am, my prayers were answered, and I had a girl. I named her Angela Lynn Hernandez. The name was already picked out. It was one of the first names I came upon from one of those name books. I didn't even have to go past the "A" s; I think it even had a little Spanish origin to it. I never did pick out a boy's name. There was not a plan "B". She was born at OHSU hospital, where I spent a couple of nights, and I have no recall of Ray seeing me after Angie was born. I'm sure he did, but I don't think I really cared about that. This was all about me, even then! This was not some sort of milestone between Ray and me of smiles and tears.

I began breast feeding and getting myself in and out of bed. At the foot of the metal frame was a hand crank. They showed me how to raise and lower the angle, telling me that I would heal faster if I did this on my own and that it was good for me. I was all for that. I enjoyed my two days away from Ray. The quiet and peace lying in my recovery bed was a small retreat. It was so nice having the nurses bring Angie in for nursing along with bedside meals. Such a new experience, kind of like royal treatment? Or maybe it was more a sense of being cared for. In my sendoff care package was a trial box of pampers, about half a dozen. I had never changed a diaper before and had to read the instructions on the pamper box.

After a couple of days in the hospital, Ray came to pick us up. I had no reason to assume that we were not going straight home if you could call it that, but I did not know where he was driving us. As he pulled into a small parking lot, I had no idea why we were there. It turned out it was the welfare office. When we parked, he said, "Go in and get welfare and food stamps, and no matter what you do, do not tell them that I am the father."

I would describe my circumstances as someone who was completely dominated and under the full control of an abuser. Not so long before this, he had promised my parents that he would never have us on welfare. I could not believe this! I did not want to go in, but I knew I had no choice. I had to do as I was told. I stepped out of the car, holding my three-day-old baby in my arms, and walked toward the building. Blocking out the duress that I was under by my abuser, I held it together, pulled open the glass door, and walked in. All I wanted to do was control my nervousness as I approached the high counter to tell them why I was there. I told myself that they did not know anything; they would have no clue that the actual father was sitting in the car forcing me to do this. I told the woman at the reception counter that I had just had this baby, and I did not know who the father was, and that I needed welfare and food stamps. They set up an appointment for me to come back, but they gave me temporary food stamps that same day. I'm sure he was pleased.

When I returned to get further benefits, I sat through a grueling intake, with most of the questions being about who may have been the father. I stalled in my answers, acting as though I was trying to recall when the likely event happened. I mentioned some parties that I had been to…a couple of made-up encounters, and the names of a few guys from high school. I felt horrible mentioning names, as I knew clearly that I was lying. My heart was pounding, and I began stressing, fearful that they would actually follow up on these accusations. I was deliberately very vague, basically played dumb, played the role. I had strict instructions and could not screw this up. The whole thing was humiliating and horribly stressful. I felt that I was a criminal, and my getaway car was just outside waiting for me to do the job, but I did get through it.

I would spend my days in the motel, learning how to take care of a baby. I had never been around babies before. I had not had much interest in them. I never wanted to babysit. One morning, as I woke up, I panicked and ran to Angie to make sure that everything was OK. I was usually awakened to get up and breastfeed, and seeing that it was already light outside, I was terrified that something may have happened to her. Why had she not awakened me by now? Thank God she was just sleeping, and I could calm down as my fears turned to relief.

I made a Thanksgiving dinner in the outdated kitchenette of our motel; it was located at the backdoor entrance and had no windows or natural light of any kind. Ray just sat in the living room after he came home from the shop, drank beer, and smoked cigarettes. Angie was a couple of weeks old by now; there would be no visitors, no phone, and absolute solitude (or solitary confinement), which was how he liked it. One afternoon, while I was in the motel alone, I heard a knock at the back door and panicked. Ray was gone, and I was terrified that anyone would know that I was there. I knew the rules. Opening the door was forbidden. I froze and hoped they would go away.

Then, there was a knocking at the front door leading out into the courtyard. I bent down low, just in case they may try to find an opening at the edge of the blind to peek through and spot me. I was frantic and beelined into the bedroom. I got down on my hands and knees to hide on the floor alongside the bed, where there was no chance that I could be seen. I remained in place and did not move until plenty of time had passed.

I learned much later that this scary visitor was my oldest brother, Steve. He told me that he had come by to see me. At the time, I was glad that I did not know that, as I would have opened it only to suffer Ray's wrath by doing so. The training was well underway, and I was following all the rules. I'm sure I was a quick learn, but who wouldn't be? Just do whatever it takes to stay out of trouble; so not to get the shit beat out of me.

The abuse continued to get worse and worse. On top of that, he was getting evicted from the motel, and we had to load up and haul out in the middle of the night so he could avoid paying up. It was the dead of winter, and he moved us into an old condemned house on the property where the shop was located. The house was a small one-bedroom that had been completely let go. The exterior was extremely weathered with peeling paint, and all the interior walls were covered from floor to ceiling with graffiti. There was no electricity or heat source available and no stove or kitchen sink. There was no bathroom sink either, and all the fixtures had been gutted from the house. I was surprised the tub was still there.

The only running water came out of the tub spout in the bathroom, and it was cold as there was no hot water heater. Ray ran long extension cords from the shop to bring in some power, then brought over a fridge from the shop and plugged it in. On a beaten-up wood table against the wall in the gutted kitchen, I set up my two-burner hotplate and electric skillet. In the center of the living room, he placed a 50-gallon drum sideways on a brick base where an old wood stove had been. He cut a square opening at one end to put wood in or whatever else he could burn and attached some ductwork to vent it out the chimney.

Next, we went to the Goodwill for drapery. The old hardware with the pull cords was still there, so we could hang them up. We found the right drapes with the metal hooks so we could pop them in place. When we got back, I quickly realized that was never the plan. I watched him in confusion. What was he doing? With a hammer in his hand, he was pounding nails through the top of the fabric and directly into the walls... permanently covering every window so you could never look out, closing me in and cutting me off from the outside world. That should have been a major red flag; he was putting up further reinforcement and barriers, protecting his prey. I returned home to load up my antique bedroom set from my old room and got a few indoor plants to make this hell hole a little nicer. I used a solid wooden cradle that was made by some woodworker. I showed him a photo from an ad of what I wanted, and it turned out to be as pretty as the picture. I'm not sure who this person was; it was probably someone getting some auto-body work done at the shop. It was made to rock from side to side and had a beautiful wood-burned flower bouquet carved into the wood at the foot. I placed it in the living room, just feet from the bedroom, and lived out each day with the prison guard just outside. It was not quite the cute little nursery adorned in pink with the graffiti-covered walls surrounding us. Our primary needs were met. We had a roof over our heads. I would try to sleep in as long as possible, only to get up for breast feeding and diaper changes. I found myself sleeping longer and longer to pass the day away, confined, with zero contact with the outside world. I did my best to play house. I found that I could get by with my small plug-in kitchen appliances for easy meals. A kitchen sink would have been so nice, but one did not exist. I used a five-gallon bucket to wash the dishes in. Ray would fill it up with hot, sudsy water from the shop and bring it in steaming. I would place the bucket in the tub, add a little cooler water, and place the washed items to the side. Then, I would use the cold running water to rinse.

I was allowed to go to my parents' once a week for a shower. Without any hot water, this was a welcome solution. It would be quite a drive to bring me, maybe that's why it was weekly and not more often. Ray would drop me off at the curb, give me about an hour or so, and would be right back to pick us up. My dad was able to see Angie for a very short visit. My mother was still not home from Dammasch. Her stay ran for several months, and she had not seen Angie yet.

The winter months wore on. Ray would come in from the shop and throw more wood on the fire… or, on occasion, he would throw rubber floor mats in as they would pile up from the cars we detailed. This really bothered me. It seemed so wrong to be burning such a thing, and the dark black smoke would back up and plume into the room. It was so upsetting watching him throwing them in…one after the other. It was scary. They burned so fast and hot that I could not help but think that he was psychotic. The violence was ramping up, too.

I was getting beaten regularly. He drank, went to a club he liked, and would come home and smack me around. His violent attacks came out of nowhere. Clearly, there was something wrong with him. He was just a madman and knew that he could violate me whenever he wanted. No one was going to know. No one was going to hear him terrorizing me.

One cold, dark night, we drove to Taco-bell for take-out. After leaving the drive-thru, without any warning or a single clue as to what I had done wrong, he started smacking me on the side of my face during the ride home. He continued his rage when we got back and went inside, beating me, yelling...accusing me of staring at a hitchhiker. I recalled someone on the road, but this was not true. I did not stare at a hitchhiker. He made things up. Did he really believe this, or was this just all part of the training program to keep me in line? I was so hurt and helpless. I cried and cried... and threw all of my taco bell into the garbage, curled up in bed in a fetal position, and cried myself to sleep. Hours later, I woke up starving and went back to the garbage to pull myself out a wrapped burrito. I sat in the dark and ate it in silence.

I lay awake many nights, just lying still... thinking, visualizing my potential plan. All I needed to do was go into the kitchen, get a knife, and kill him while he lay in his sleep. So quick and simple! I hated him and wanted to get back at him. I lay there, trying to will myself the courage to do it. If I just keep the focus, maybe this could be an answer to finally putting an end to this nightmare. I thought long and hard about this, wondering if the ability would come to me and if I could pull this off. I could not. I did not have the capacity to do it. During one of his horrific, violent rages, he started breaking things, smashing up the house. Nothing was off limits. He grabbed my antique mirror that went to my vanity set and, with both hands, raised it high above his head. Using all the force he could, smashed it down onto the footboard of my bed. The beveled glass mirror shattered into pieces and scattered everywhere. He continued slamming it down, over and over, until the exquisite frame was now in several splintered chunks. As I watched in terror, I was crushed and crying uncontrollably. It was irreparable. I adored my bedroom set...something that I had from my previous life. It was all that I owned.

Another time, he heaved a full dozen raw eggs across the kitchen, breaking them everywhere. As he chased me and ran through the room, he slipped flat on his back and landed on the runny egg yolk. This just escalated his rage further. He raised his foot in the air, turned slightly sideways, and karate-kicked the front of the TV. His shoe went through the glass, shattering it into a million pieces and falling to the floor. All of this happened within minutes, as though he was possessed. The biggest sign that he had clearly lost it was when he tried to kick over the 50-gal drum we used for our fireplace. With the same sideways karate pose, he kicked and kicked and could not push it off of the brick. I was so relieved that he could not do it. I just stood and watched in panic, knowing that if he had been successful, he would have burned the house down.

Nothing was stopping him; he was a human Category 5 tornado and would take out everything in his path. He heaved my potted plants across the living room, breaking the ceramic pots as they hit the wall with the dirt flying everywhere. I ran to Angie's cradle so I could brush the filth off of her. Crying hysterically, I wished that I could be heard. If only someone would show up and come to my rescue. Anyone. But I also knew that my wishes would never come true. No one was going to know or witness his violence or, like a lonesome tree falling in the woods, no one would hear the sound.

Whenever we went to the grocery store, or any store for that matter, he would always make sure that we went through a female checker. In the event that we had a male clerk, I knew to look down and never look at him. Otherwise, it was surely grounds for beating me. I was fully conscious of my actions. I would try to keep my head down wherever we went and monitor my surroundings in case there was something in my view that would set him off. By this point, I was fully trained on how I needed to behave to avoid the consequences and how I was to act to avoid the next beating.

While standing in the checkout line at a store holding Angie, a very sweet, old man peeked at her and asked me how old she was. He was just being nice, and of course, I thought nothing of it. I had no idea that this would be a new violation. When we returned home, he started beating me. He said that the only reason the old man was asking me anything about Angie was because he wanted to look at my boobs! This beating was one of the most brutal; he kicked me over and over as I lay curled up on the floor, pulling my knees to my chest and tucking my face, crying my heart out, knowing there was nothing that I could do to protect myself. I had as much power as a rag doll and had not been beaten to this degree before. Every time he kicked, he did it with so much force that I would pee on the floor. I felt self-conscious and tried my hardest to hold it in, but he was kicking me way too hard. The notion that I felt shame! The insanity of this! I was getting kicked by this vicious animal, and I felt that somehow, there was something wrong with me. That I should be able to have full control of my bodily functions so as to not embarrass myself.

He stood me up and started strangling me. I was scared to death, feeling the tight hold and pressure on my neck as I could no longer take in a full breath. How far was he going to take this? My life was in his hands, literally. Thankfully, he let go. I tried to enjoy the little milestones, watching Angie learn to roll over and sit up and see the look in her eyes while I held up plastic-colored objects. I would prop her up in a chair and support her with pillows to her sides so she could watch me while I was in the kitchen or while I was in my prison. I also had a little Chihuahua named Taco. She was so sweet and tiny and would sleep all the way under the covers, down at my feet. Unfortunately, one afternoon, she was stolen from the car.

While I spent my days in lockdown, I was not allowed to step outside, prop open a curtain, or have a landline. I literally was captive, and it was not on my mind to go anywhere at all. Where would I go anyway? My weekly shower was what I had to look forward to. Each day was joyless. I think it's a slow process, but when an abuser starts closing in the walls around you, you slowly die out. You're completely unaware of this change in you, as this person is re-making your world to be smaller and smaller. You disconnect from your past. You adapt to your circumstances. You are under the rule of your owner and learn your boundaries. He is not a loving caregiver wanting what is best for you. This abuser is only serving himself, shaping and grooming his chattel. As you're shrinking spirit contracts to your reality, you lose vision. I no longer thought beyond the day. I think you succumb to your circumstances, and you live one day at a time.

I never let on to anyone about the abuse. I hid every bit of it. Ray would often threaten that if I ever tried to leave him, he would have children's services take Angie away from me so fast my head would spin. This was enough to keep me in line and do as I was told. He terrified me. I believed what he was telling me. I believed that there would be no way for me to keep her on my own. I resigned myself to the idea that I had to have him in order to not have her taken away. This fear he placed in me kept me going along with whatever he wanted.

On one occasion, he came in the front door from the shop while I was inside caring for Angie, and he went ballistic as the door was unlocked. I had stepped onto the porch to shake out a rug and did not lock the door when I stepped in. I did not even think about it. I told him why I had stepped out on the porch, and he was furious and began yelling. He was raging with anger, letting me know that he knew what I really was up to. He said the reason I stepped out on the porch was that I really just wanted to get a look at the guys working over at the Chevron station and that I wanted them to see me.

Ray was a criminal, and he used me in any way he could. When Angie was just a few months old, another one of his money-making schemes was in full action. We made the rounds every day to Homebase (now Home Depot) and filled up the diaper bag with stolen tools. We went from one store to the next, a daily routine. As we entered the store, we headed directly to the tool department with baby in tow and the diaper bag hanging off my shoulder. Ray placed the items into the bag, and we walked out, filling the trunk with our haul. I was not along when he sold off the goods each day. I was not needed for that. I imagine he knew plenty of takers.

We never got caught. At the Montgomery Ward store at Mall 205, that nearly changed. Walking to the glass doors to leave with the bag of goods, a swarm of security people came out of nowhere and surrounded us. I froze in place. I stood holding the bag, literally. He had made me a part of this. They would not know that I was under his daily control, that he made the plan to go to the store that day, and that he made the decisions. We were busted, and I knew that I would be going down with him. There would be no getting around that fact. We were asked to remove the items that he had stolen from the bag, and he took it from my shoulder to open it up for the security agents, but it was empty. There was nothing in it. It turned out that Ray had spotted them ahead of time. I did not know it, but he had removed the items from the bag before we attempted to leave the store. I had no idea. I stood there in disbelief, knowing that we had taken things. The security guard was very angry. He told Ray that he saw him stealing the goods and demanded that he tell them where the items were. He just denied the accusition being levied against him, and we left the store.

Ray did auto-body repair and paint work, the trade he learned while incarcerated. I was trained on how to mask cars to get them ready for paint. This was something that I was very good at. I was very meticulous and detailed, applying the tape to avoid paint going where it shouldn't. He taught me how to water sand the entire car after he did the body repairs, the final step before painting. My working for zero pay should have been another financial benefit toward the overhead. It seemed that he had plenty of work. I don't know why we struggled so much financially. We lived in a condemned house with rats. No rent there! I never received a dime of my own personal spending money, slave labor. Then, to top that off, he forced us on the dole and never made a single child-support payment to his ex.

I did get a little resourceful and would sneak small change off the dresser and hide it, tucking it away for weeks until I could splurge. I bought myself a three-tiered natural wicker plant stand from Fred Meyer; each tier was round and about 10 inches across. I'm not sure how I was able to do this without getting in some kind of trouble, but that is what it took to have something.

Spring was coming, and I was almost done nursing. He began talking to me about his next latest, greatest scheme on how to make really good money. Basically, he wanted to prostitute me. He described how this would be done and how he would get the Johns from the local bars. It was all so simple. Most of his spin was all about easy money, trying to motivate me with this financial opportunity. He rattled on about what he wanted me to do, which was all so disgusting. I didn't want anything to do with it.

The night had arrived, and he exercised his full control. I waited in the car, sitting in the dark in a very large parking lot at a nightclub he frequented. He brought a John out to the car from the bar. I lay in the backseat with this stranger on top of me. I saw that Ray was on his knees in the front seat, masturbating while he watched. A nightmare. Other times, he drove me over and dropped me off around a seedy industrial area until a John would approach. Ray would prepare me and give me full instructions as to what to say. Something about being short on my rent seemed to work. A blow-job was $20. I obviously got this whole relationship very wrong; I believed that I was entering into a life where I would be looked after and taken good care of. That is what was promised me at my parent's table on the day I revealed my pregnancy. Not so. This new life came at a heavy price.

The shop burned down. I have no idea what started the fire, and I believe that it originated from a car inside the shop. The extent of the fire and all the damage in the shop destroyed all the electrical wiring, cutting off the electric power to the condemned house. We had no resources, no credit, and zero cash. Clearly, no friends that he could turn to in times of need. He started to put this all on me, and he was relentless. He needed money. He forced me to get us some help. Money from my parents would not be possible, though I was able to get them to ask my grandfather for a small loan. This proved very difficult. I really hated being put in this situation. I felt absolutely horrible. I never wanted anyone else's money. All I could do was continue to assure all of them of Ray's promise that he would pay it back. My grandfather did not want to give us any money. He did not believe that Ray would ever pay him back, and my grandparents also thought that I should put Angie up for adoption. But my grandfather relented, and I got the money. Of course, my grandfather was right. He never gave them back a dollar. With my grandfather's generosity, we could now look for an apartment. We were making application at the Villa Felicia apartments on 158th and Stark. I remember the woman talking with Ray, and I could tell that she had serious reservations. He would have had to smooth-talk her, as I'm sure things did not look good on paper. Maybe she felt sorry for us. I was sitting there with a four-month-old baby. He had nothing, and if he had any credit at all, I'm sure it was horrible. I believe it was out of the goodness of her heart that she let us have the keys.

By late March, I was no longer living in the house of nightmares. The nightmare would continue, but the physical change was a new beginning. The apartment was up on the 2nd level with beautiful light coming in through the front picture window. Seeing the light of the day, along with it flowing into the room, brought me some real joy. The best part was that Ray did not nail the curtains up. Thank goodness we were up on the 2nd floor, or he probably would have. We moved a few things in. It was sparse. My brother became a woodworker with my father and made me a beautiful coffee table that sat in the middle of the living room, a stand-alone showpiece. I placed my 3-tiered wicker plant stand at the window. I just loved my new spot; it was such a huge step up from the ghetto house. Standing in the middle of the room and seeing outside, taking in the tops of the Douglas fir trees, was overwhelming. However, this freedom to gaze outside would once again prove to be another huge disobedient transgression.

Ray was ordered by the court to be on Antabuse. His daily drinking and DUI's were catching up to him and getting him in trouble with the law. The crazy thing about all of this was that he continued to drink. He was required to show up three times per week at a local pharmacy, where they gave him a small amount of liquid in a cup and watched him drink it. I guess the rules or the orders did not apply to him. He was going to beat the system. After buying a short case of cold beers, he said the trick was that you had to drink the first beer really, really slowly, and then you were good. I think he actually thought that he could figure out a way to keep alcohol in his life. I could see that his crazy idea was not working. He would drink, and his skin would turn super red, and his eyes became extremely bloodshot. After a few beers and shortness of breath, he dropped to the floor and passed out. I left him in place and negotiated around his lifeless body.

During one of these drinking occasions, while on Antabuse, he went into one of his routine rages at the apartment. I was just minding my own business on a sunny afternoon while he drank when he started yelling at me and accusing me of watching some young boys, probably around ten years old. There was a very small parking area that you could look down onto from the living room window where a couple of boys were riding their bicycles around in circles. As usual, he concocted some idea in his head that I could not diffuse, sending him into a full-blown rage. This was a bad one. He was heavily intoxicated, completely red, and had trouble breathing. He started coming at me, attacking me, and chasing me around the apartment as I ran wherever I could to avoid the beatings. His level of rage felt like "The Shining," as though I was in a horror movie. I was absolutely terrified; he began dragging me by my hair down the hall as I was screaming my lungs out. I prayed someone would hear me this time and come to my rescue. I continued screaming as loud as I could, expecting at any moment help would arrive at the door. He pulled me up from the floor just outside the bathroom and shoved me backward as hard as he could. My back slammed hard into the wall, and I broke the towel bar off. I was crying hysterically and could barely breathe. He was completely out of control. I pleaded and begged for him to take me to my parents' house. Crying uncontrollably, I kept saying...over and over...please, please, just take me to my parents. I could not take this; I was so broken and desperate. I was waiting for someone to come to the apartment door. Surely this time would be different. I was living at an apartment complex, not in isolated seclusion. Someone had to hear me. This time would surely be different.

I was wrong. No one came.

I have no idea how or why, but Ray drove me over to my parents. Did my begging him, over and over, win out? I do not know. I'm sure he thought that this time would be no different than any other time I was allowed to visit. He would just come back later and pick me up. He had no idea. Actually, I don't believe I did either.

A blessing awaited. Ray dropped me curbside at my parents, and with Angie in tow, I went inside. It was the weekend, so as luck would have it, my dad was home sitting in his easy chair in the living room. Someone was there, maybe not at the door, as I had prayed many times, but *there* all the same. I could not hold all of this in any longer, and fell apart. I was hysterical and could not get myself to stop crying. My dad demanded to know what was wrong. He had never spoken up about much before, but I could tell that he really meant it. I could sense his genuine concern. He wanted to know what was going on. At this point, I had nothing to lose. I did not hold back. I told him everything. I told him about every beating. I did not want to miss a thing. I wanted to get it all out, every last detail of all the abuse that I had completely hidden. I did not want to cover for him anymore and did not care that I was going to expose him. I was having an emotional breakdown and hit a breaking point.

I had not gone over there with a plan of any kind; I just wanted to get to a safe place. I just wanted to get away from him. After I had finished telling my dad everything with my mom in the background, my dad spoke up immediately and said, "Brenda, you are not leaving this house!"

This changed everything. He spoke up and said those words so firmly. I could not believe what I just heard. He meant it! He did love me! Regardless of my father's lack of demonstrative affection, he was there for me when I needed him the most.

My life had become intolerable and terrifying. Ray was an abuser, and I was his victim. This day would become the end of my nightmare, the end of my life with Ray. I was so grateful to my dad for speaking up and forever thankful for his giving me a way out. I never looked back. I received the help of my older brother, Steve, to load up a truck with my things at the apartment...and got out forever.

I did not have to stay with Ray to keep my baby! His complete bullshit did not have a hold on me any longer. He lost!!

Ray continued to try to make contact. He would phone my parents' home to get me on the line, asking me to come back. If my dad answered, he would not let him speak with me. On a couple of occasions, I would pick up…listening to him in despair, I would let him come by and pick me up to talk. We would just drive around or go to a park. By this time, he was drinking heavily. He no longer had the shop and was living in his car.

His calls and efforts to get me to change my mind all failed. He would use pressure tactics to coerce me, to get me back with the old "if I can't have you, no one can" approach, trying to place fear in me. None of this was going to work. He then told me that he tried to kill himself by sitting in a running car in a closed garage. This likely did happen, but I also think he used it as another manipulation, a last-ditch effort to get my attention, for me to feel sorry for him so I would come back. So crafty, in a sick way… or the way of a con man. This perpetrator was saying, "How important you are" and "How much you mean to me," which was what one wanted to hear or-believe.

This was the trap that had put me in this cycle of abuse. Falling for another con. On one call, he let me know that he had been arrested for assault and described the entire incident as what had happened. Ray was a very heavy drinker, and he became extremely violent when he drank. On this particular afternoon, he said he was in his car at an apartment complex and that a group of guys yelled down at him, saying, "Hey, why don't you drive your car right?" These three individuals were up above on a balcony, looking down over the parking lot. Ray jumped out of his car, broke a quart bottle of beer on the street to make a weapon and be-lined to the upper deck, and attacked every one of them. Brutally striking them with the sharp, broken glass end of the bottle. He told me that he had cut open a guy's face from the top of his forehead to the bottom of his chin. Charges were now pending against him.

Several months had passed, and then Ray phoned to tell me that he had been sentenced to five years in Federal prison in Colorado. I recall feeling a little sorry for him at the time, but then I quickly came to my senses and started realizing the reality of this. Five years!! That seemed like a lifetime in which he would no longer be out there, trying to make contact, phoning me to see him, and having to listen to his pleas to reconsider. I felt that a constant threat over my life had been completely removed. The sky cleared, and I was free to live my daily life, come and go, without the underlying worry that he might try to find me and continue to terrorize me.

CHAPTER TWO

On My Own

After about three months of sleeping on the sofa at my parents, my best friend Tammie found a cute little house for rent on 80th and Fremont in N.E. Portland and asked me to be her roommate. It was a small 2-bedroom one level home with a laundry room. How great! A perfect little start for me. We split the $195 per month rent and the electric bill. I would remain living there for five years. Tammie moved on after a year or so. I was more comfortable with a sense of stability and made this place our home. Unfortunately, it came at the cost of needing roommates.

I quickly found employment at Dehen Knitting Co. I met directly with Mr. Dehen in his office about some work. I must have mentioned that I really did not know what to do or where to turn for work… and that I could probably pick up a waitressing job. I clearly remember, and will never forget, his telling me that waitressing was a dead-end job. I admired Mr. Dehen, respected what he had to say, and trusted his advice. I'm sure I need much more guidance than what jobs to avoid, but that was not his job. So, I decided to take a regular job in a factory. My Mom found me some childcare through the classifieds located close-in S.E. Portland, which was a big help, I have to say.

I drove Angie to the sitter early in the morning. It was difficult to bring her in and drop her off while she was crying and reaching her hands out to me. Jeannie helped me not to worry ("Just go ahead and leave…Everything will be fine."), and I rushed off to get to Old Town and clock in by 7 am. After my relationship ended with Ray, he did provide me with and old 1963 Rambler, a critical necessity in order to gain employment. I worked in an old industrial building down in the basement area, tying on cones of yarn as the knitting machines churned out yards and yards of sweater fabric. The room was windowless, with concrete walls and floors and shop lighting that could not replace the lack of natural light. We clocked our time cards in and out for two 15-minute breaks, and I took my

30-minute lunch in another windowless room. I took my brown bag up the narrow, creaky wood stairs to the small break room with a couple of banquet tables and a few metal chairs. I learned quickly that I hated factory work, the biggest reason being that I couldn't stand not seeing the light of day. I quit after about 6 months.

Tammie found out how we could get Fake I.D.s. I think it was just an ad in a magazine or something? For only five dollars, you could mail away to a company called the U.S. Press a photo of yourself along with the City and State, name, and birthdate that you would like to use. I sent in a small school years photo from high school, and chose Portland, Maine, along with the name Brenda Lee Johnson and a birth year, making me 21. After receiving the laminated I.D., we took it to the DMV to get official Oregon I.D.s.

Now we could hit the dance clubs and listen to live music downtown. We dressed it up in our vintage finds from the thrift stores; I wore rhinestone jewelry and got help with my hair to pull it off. We were a couple of party girls on the loose. I had just turned 17 and was not aware that I would be heading into more than two decades of alcohol abuse. After breaking away and getting on my own, I continued to gravitate to the partiers, the drinking crowd. That was definitely where I felt I fit in best, or to put it a different way...where I could find an escape. I'm sure many of the others had their own issues. Misery loves company. I felt most comfortable with the misfits. They might accept me, as opposed to the educated "Suits." I was way too screwed up for that demographic.

After Dehen Knitting Co, I took whatever I could get on the job front. I commuted downtown again, this time to the Federal Building. I did light secretarial for the US Marine Corp. recruiting dept. My job description must have been very uneventful, as I don't recall exactly what I did. A gunnery Sergeant took an interest in me, but it ended as quickly as it began. He took me along on an official business trip he was attending for Military officers...I think in Seattle. When I returned to work the following week, there was quite the gossip going on. He was in really big trouble with his job for taking me along. This was a very serious violation, and he was very close to being terminated.

I learned that he was married, which could better explain the seriousness of his offense. I took the fall and was let go from my job. I remember clearly that he tried to somehow assure me that I was very important to him by saying, "Love is not something that you turn off like a light switch." Men can be such manipulators. I never saw him again.

I signed up for dance lessons with a promotion offering ten lessons for only $10 dollars. Such a brilliant marketing campaign, bringing in a steady flow of wannabes, hoping to make their mark on the dance floor. Disco was the rage, and Dance world was in its heyday, packed with people wanting to learn some moves. It was similar to Arthur Murray, but this dance studio was going after a new market of young night-clubbers. Dancing under the sparkling disco ball with all the stunning rainbow colors bouncing off of everything was magical. Line dancing was also a favorite, made popular by the movie Saturday night fever with John Travolta.

Just as I began my first few classes, I was offered a job. Dance world was hiring dance instructors. We would not only learn the latest dances; we would earn pay and commission. I wasn't expecting this to turn into a job opportunity and jumped at the chance. I needed a job after being let go from the Marine Corp. position. I would be trained and become part of what was called the "front department." The individuals coming in on the promotional offer needed instructors to fill the demand. The training was a mix of sales, as well as being taught basic ballroom. I had to learn each Dance - the Cha-cha, Salsa, Tango, and even the Waltz -but also learn to do them backward since I would have to teach them to my male students and lead them into the moves. Every session was an hour long and had a name; the first one was "Make a Friend." We were very scripted. We were taught every word that we were to say, enticing them into buying a several thousand-dollar dance package. I was naturally good at my job, and I sold everyone. The only problem was that when they showed back up for their 11th hour, we had to introduce them to their next instructors, the instructors belonging to the "back department" who would run out their hours. Most would reluctantly continue, but I did have some cancel the entire purchase. They thought they were buying the next six months with me. Of course, this was a huge bummer for me because I would, therefore, not earn my commission! All that work. Selling the dance packages was what we were there for.

I took Angie to her daycare as usual, and would park on the east side of the river where I could hop a bus into downtown to save on parking expenses. I really enjoyed this job as I loved to dance and had a little knack for sales. The older "back department" male instructors would waltz me around the ballroom floor when we had breaks between clients. Such a highlight to have some real fun dancing. The teaching part was just a job. As I learned more, a few of us would hit the local dance clubs, where I would be hoisted up above their heads and twirled around wearing my Danskin leotard and matching skirt.

All this ended abruptly when another nightmare unfolded.

CHAPTER THREE

Major Scare

The morning of July 12, 1978, began like any other, except this particular morning something was not right. When I went in to change Angie's diaper, my roommate and I noticed that her right eyelid was completely swollen, and she felt slightly warm. I was very rushed for work, so I gave her some Liquiprin, dressed her, and dropped her at her sitter, Jeannie's.

At 3:30 pm I received an emergency call from her in the middle of my dance lesson and ran to the phone. Angie was much worse. She told me to come get her and take her to the doctor right away. I hung up the phone, started crying, and ran to get my purse. I immediately ran to the bus, then to my car...picked her up, and arrived at Kaiser by 4:15 pm.

Her regular doctor was not in, so she was seen by another doctor on duty. As she was being looked at, I noticed that both her ears were draining. He checked them and said, "Bingo." I asked if her eye was related to the ear infection, and he said that, somehow, the germ had spread to her eye. By now, her swollen eye-lid had completely grown shut, and it looked like a ping pong ball was underneath it. The entire eyelid was a dark, purplish color.

He prescribed Amoxicillin and something else for her eye. When I got home, I gave her both medications and put her down. She seemed completely out of it, with no energy whatsoever. She slept till about 8:30 pm, and when she woke, she was very fussy and whining. I brought her into my room and lay her on my bed, then went into the kitchen to bring her some cereal. By the time I was back in my bedroom, she had conked out again.

I took a bath, then got right back to check on her. I noticed she was breathing very rapidly, and it looked like her chest was vibrating. I felt her heart, and it felt considerably fast. Then I felt her whole body, and she was literally burning up. I laid my cheek down on her tummy, and it burned me. I knew things were not good and that she was in bad shape. I was feeling so uneasy as to what to do, and I quickly started looking through the phonebook to find her regular doctor's phone number…Anna Chapman. I immediately called her, and she answered, after telling her what was going on, she told me to take her temp and call her right back. After a couple of attempts, I could not manage to get a reading. I called her back, and she said that she would be right over. She arrived in about two minutes. As luck (or divinity) would have it, she lived right around the corner. She took Angie's temp and did not communicate with me what it read. She just said in a calm way, "Run some cold water in the tub right away." I asked if she found her temp, and she replied she did. Then asked her what it read, and she answered 106 degrees. I could not believe it. She asked me to get the Sunnyside Kaiser number while she got Angie ready for the tub. I handed her the phone and number; she told me to continue bathing her. She was on the phone with Kaiser for only a minute and ran back, saying never mind the bath; get her ready to go to the Hospital… she needs to be seen right away.

Everything was quickly becoming urgent. We towel-dried her, got her nightie on, and we were out the door. I drove my car while she held Angie. At about 11 pm, I pulled up in front of the Hospital to let her out and go in. I entered the Hospital and followed her down the hall to the room that she was taken to; the attending doctor said that I would have to leave the room while he did a spinal tap. He explained it was a test to see if she had any fluid in her spinal column that was cloudy-looking. I headed to the waiting area, signed some paper work, then peeked through Angie's door. The doctor was taking off her nightie, and the nurse turned me away. Anna and I walked back to the waiting area. I could hear Angie screaming all the way through the long corridor and out to where we were waiting. After about 10 minutes, the doctor came running out yelling, "Anna, it's positive," and continued running past us. She then explained to me that Angie had Meningitis and would have to be hospitalized. She explained the fluid they found meant that it had spread throughout her entire body. She would need to be placed on antibiotics, and they took many blood samples to grow the virus to determine the type. The doctor explained to me that the germ had formed a pus covering her brain and entered her spinal column. He then said that the first 24 hours were the most critical, and he did not know if she would make it or not!

I could not believe what I was hearing. Up to this point, I believed that this would be a night in the Hospital and nothing more. That was shocking enough, but I'd felt that everything would be fine. Now, complete panic was setting in as my mind started racing with extreme fear. My entire life, as I visualized it, disappeared. I could see nothing, only a murky white fog with nothing in it! It was completely empty. I had no one! It all ended. I knew I would not be able to handle that. In my mind, I was packing my bags. I would be going to Dammasch State Mental Hospital. I would not have been able to go on. I would have nothing to live for.

Anna led me to the room where Angie was transferred to. I phoned my parents asking if they could come to be with us for a while. I was an emotional wreck and did not know what to do with myself. The thought of her dying was intolerable. I loved her so much. I told Anna that I had never, ever had a thought or regret of having her, no matter what I heard from family or friends.

I spent the entire night and the next day by her side, watching her lying there, not knowing if she was going to make it or not. Not knowing from minute to minute what to expect. They asked me to leave the room a few times as they had to re-stick a new I.V. into another vein. I refused to leave, and I felt that I was a comfort to her by being there. I stood by her side hour after hour, holding her hand and praying, telling her that it would be alright and that I loved her more than anything in the world. I rested in a chair off and on while she slept, but as soon as I heard the slightest whimper, I was back up to comfort her and begging God to save her.

The next day was looking positive; she was still alive, and her temp was coming down. I learned that one of the first indicators of survival is when your body temperature starts to lower. The doctor who had seen her when we arrived stayed the night at the Hospital for her. She was so critical. He was surprised the next morning that she was still alive. The doctor who tended to her the previous day prescribing Amoxicillin showed up early morning as well. I had to think his misdiagnosis would have made him feel awful. I also had to think that his diagnosis was border line malpractice. She was sent home at near death. I was so young at the time, mostly timid, and never confrontational, so I did not question her care.

I continued visiting her twice daily, and she began a liquid diet of soup, Jell-O, milk, and apple juice. I fed her at dinner time and watched T.V. with her. She was getting better day by day, and her eye was looking better. I was told that she would probably be OK, although there was still a possibility that something could go wrong later. They mentioned that she could have been a better-than-average learner and now a less-than-average one or a very slow learner. (By 1st grade, she was placed in the TAG program for talented and gifted.)

The day that Angie got sick, I quit my job and did not return. I received my last paycheck from Dance World and bought Angie lots of new clothes and toys. I painted her room a very light, pale yellow and hung-up pretty pictures. Then lined a wall of open shelves with cheerful contact paper, placing the toys and arranging stuffed animals on them.

My mother and youngest brother, Chris, drove me to pick her up. She seemed as good as new. She was in the Hospital for a total of 14 days, a brush with death at only a year and a half. I've always said that she came through with flying colors. I never noticed any repercussions; she was happy and loving and better with strangers.

This is the story as I wrote it, July 1978...today at age 63, I can still remember it vividly. I recall my prayers that night; I am so very grateful that my prayers were answered.

CHAPTER FOUR

Tough Blow

After Angie recovered from spinal Meningitis and returned home in July of 1978, I was all set to begin the fall term at Portland Community College. After meeting with the career counselor, who went over all of the Associate Degree programs available, I decided on Real Estate. Nothing else appealed to me. I hated science class and had to transfer out of biology as it was way over my head. Anything related to the health and the medical field was definitely out. Everything Real Estate was a perfect fit for me. I was eligible for the BEOG Basic Educational Opportunity Grant, and because I was a single-mom and already on my own, they waived the requirement to get my GED. I registered for all of my classes, got my books, and was very excited for school to begin and start another chapter of my life. My job prospects looked very grim, and I could not have made a better choice than school to better myself. On a very warm, sunny, late afternoon, feeling sun-bronzed and care-free coming home from sunbathing at the river, I had the radio on, my windows rolled down, and my blonde hair blowing every which way... which made me stand out, unfortunately, as a target. It was the weekend, and I was anxious to get home and clean up before going out. I was just about to approach my house when a black gentleman pulled up alongside my car and asked if I was interested in doing a line of coke.

Great, a little pick me up. I was cool with that and invited him in. This was a very quick encounter, a line of coke. That was it. I was rushed by then and told him that I had to get ready to go out, and he left.

The following morning, I was getting ready to leave and pick Angie up at my parents. I was actually very pleased with myself, heading out to get her early… and what do you know, there he was! Rather shocked and a little confused as to how it was that he was right there should have caused me some concern. I was always unsuspecting, getting myself into awful situations. He said that he had something he wanted to show me. He seemed very excited to share something with me, and of course, I took the bait. I let him come in, and he started to work his magic. He talked fast and had a lot of enthusiasm about this game he wanted to show me. "Hey, hey...check this out!"

Somewhat animated and hyper, he sat down on the sofa and placed three bottle caps in front of him on the coffee table. As he shuffled them around, he placed a small bean under one of them and asked if I knew where it was and, if so, point to the correct bottle cap. Well, of course, I knew where it was...what a stupid question. I pointed the cap, and voila! There it was. He tried to act a little surprised, as though I was somehow really good at this new game that I had just learned. Well, if you know anything about the shell game this got really bad really quick!

He asked if I wanted to play again, and he would give me $20 bucks if I won. My mind was quickly thinking how stupid this guy was. "Yes, of course, I want to play again."

What do you know, I won twenty bucks. I could not believe this. How awesome...I was absolutely thrilled at my good fortune. Then he raised the amount I could win; the catch was that I had to put something up of value to play the next round. Sure, no problem... I told him I would put up an Oriental rug. Same as before, I pointed to the winning cap. He turned it over and there was nothing under it. What? OK, he is just playing a joke on me. He then asked what else I had, and we could play again…if I won, I would get everything back. Whoa, what a relief! Thank God there was a solution as sudden panic now was setting in. Little did I know, I was in over my head. I went and got my expensive AE-1 Cannon camera and placed it on the table…OK, here we go, game on. Well, what do you think happened? You're right. I lost.

By now, my heart was pounding fast, and I was starting to get seriously worried. What was this guy doing? I was trying to think about what else I could put up to save the day. As I scanned around my house and couldn't spot anything that would do, I remembered one last item: a wedding band set from my relationship with Ray, Angie's dad. I would put that up. I just needed to get this right, and I would be fully restored and able to get on with my day.

No, no, no! This can't be! I was screaming inside. I lost again. I was terrified. I had no idea what was happening. Or I did and could not accept this reality.

He was not kidding and started taking everything out of my house. I was an emotional wreak. What the hell had I done?

I wanted to fix what I had just done. The only thing he told me was that I could buy my stuff back, and he gave me his number.

In the days that followed, I really felt that I did not have it in me to start school. I was truly crushed, and full defeat was setting in. Things were not working out for me, and the weight of this was taking over. I was definitely at a crossroads. I had one of two choices. I visualized school…and making that my choice, and then the alternative: just give it up. *You cannot fix the mess that you have just made.* Within minutes of processing each choice, my last bit of inspiration ruled the day. I have got to move forward! Followed by, you have got to do this! You cannot let the outcome of this appalling event ruin your plans. As I thought through this, the choice of moving forward started to lift me up and gave me strength. I was shattered inside and discovered that the best cure and way to repair this screw-up was to "back up and get a running jump." That is literally the dialogue I had in my head. I had one of two choices, and thankfully, it would be College!

I had not fully let this incident go, and made an appointment with an attorney to get some assistance. I went to the Multnomah County courthouse fully expecting that I would have some rights and be advised of some legal recourse available to me. I sat in a small room with a gentleman who patiently sat and listened. I spent a considerable amount of time explaining the entire ordeal and giving him all of the details. After I finished, he replied that this was not a criminal matter and there was nothing that could be done. Hearing this was hard to believe, and it seemed like a slam dunk. I was clearly the victim here.

This was my first experience with a conman. Well, I guess I should say, another type of conman. I was one hundred percent not prepared for this one. I was very naïve and clueless that there were really bad people out there. I had no filters, no awareness, really, and lived without any guard rails. I was so vulnerable to being taken advantage of. This had been a different kind of predator and I was easy prey. Besides being petite, I was always nice and friendly, never being a threat to my victimizer.

I accepted my fate. And leapt forward.

CHAPTER FIVE

Not My Time

In the wee hours of the morning, I came to at Woodland Park hospital. My roommate was there in the room standing over me. It was December 2, 1979. As I started opening my eyes, trying to adjust them to all the bright light, I could see her face looking down over mine. Struggling to think and come back to reality, I heard her say to me, "Bren, you were in an accident."

I felt so out of it and struggled to comprehend what she had just said. I then asked her if I was driving, and she replied, "Yes."

The shock! The fear! I had no idea what she was talking about. How could this be? I could not believe this. We were just at a pool table together at a local pub. I was celebrating the end of my fall term from PCC with her, and I just had a full set of beautiful acrylic nails put on at a nail salon in downtown Portland. Nails had just come on the scene, and I loved them. I went to Nails on Broadway, which was the first Nail Salon to open in Portland. I had always wished that I had strong, pretty nails, and with acrylic nails, that was forever solved. I was so excited to step out with my roomy and party: school done, new nails and a need to escape. Finals week would begin the following week, and I was all ready to take my exams, but first, girls' night out!

I learned from the paramedics that rescued me, and also from the police reports what had happened. A few fuzzy details had emerged that fateful night that I was on the road. I recall being a little upset with my roommate that she had invited a guy over to our house from the pub. We had made a pact together before going out: no hooking up. We would have no guys over. Well, with this violation of our agreement, I would settle the score, and in the blur, I stormed out to go to an after-hours nightclub up on 102nd and Halsey…a discotheque called the Great Gatsby, not more than a couple miles away. I was only 19 years old, but I had my trusty fake I.D. This dance club was very popular, and I went there often, so not a surprise that I would be going there. I had not had my car very long and was very new to driving a stick shift, especially when intoxicated! This was an accident waiting to happen.

According to the police reports, I was traveling from Fremont, heading south on 92nd Ave. towards Halsey. It was a very dark, rainy, winter night on this two-lane highway as I was reported speeding and driving on the wrong side of the road. The Portland police were in pursuit to pull me over when I veered off of the road, which had a soft shoulder and no sidewalks, crashing into someone's front yard a block or so before reaching Halsey St. Good thing. Reaching Halsey could have only made things much worse, as it was a much busier four-lane highway.

Because the police were behind me, they were able to watch all of this go down and call for an ambulance as my car plowed into a very large tree and then smashed into a sailboat. I must have been sprung from the car and hurled. The paramedics who arrived on the scene said that they had found me 50 feet away from my car, lying face down in the dirt.

The police spotting me that night was another blessing or miracle that I could not be more grateful for. Yes, I was in big trouble and got my first DUI, but without such grace, I would have just laid there and died on that cold December night.

With my roommate still consoling me as I lay in the Hospital, I was slowly realizing the gravity of all that had happened. I was somewhat numb to it all, as though I had yet to fully awaken from a dream. It was all so hard to accept; I could not believe what I was responsible for doing, what I had done to myself. Such an abrupt turn of events from drinking and partying, happily intoxicated, to being hospitalized and injured in several places. The black-out made it seem as though everything happened in the blink of an eye, from a pool table to a hospital bed. Thank God I was in good hands and not still lying on the frozen ground half a mile away. The nightmare! How easily could it all have gone that way?

As I was trying to assess the full situation, my left hand bumped into something very hard and foreign, and I felt this thick, solid cast covering my left leg to the top of my thigh. Apparently, I broke both bones in my shin and, for whatever reason, needed my entire leg casted. I'm not sure how long it takes to have a cast put on, but it became clearer how out of it I must have been. I was unconscious or passed out during the whole process. My forehead was covered in bandages, and a cut on my chin was all stitched up. I don't know if there is a difference between being knocked out with head trauma or if I was passed out due to too much alcohol. Probably both?

The paramedics had placed a neck brace around my neck at the scene, I'm sure standard procedure, as they discovered me filthy dirty with a bloody forehead and fir needles matted into my hair. I lay motionless and flat on my back, sleeping and sobering up for hours until I would be transferred to Sunnyside Kaiser, where they would discover that I had broken my neck. I suspect that I landed head-first as I was ejected from my car. I have no knowledge to this day of how this all unfolded. My car was completely totaled, the entire driver's door was severely smashed in, and the windshield was crushed down on top of the driver's seat. Seeing my car, a pile of wreckage in my driveway after I was released from the Hospital, was quite a revelation and made no sense. I would have had to be tossed out before all of this final damage occurred. My brush with death.

After completing several layers of X-rays of my neck, finally, they were able to find a small crack. Locating the break required scan after scan, as the imaging had to be done in slices and took some time to find. This resulted in my being placed in traction for seven dreadful days. None of this was good news.

The concern of the doctors was mostly not knowing how I was going to heal. They explained to me that I may not heal well and they may need to fuse my neck. This would mean that I would have only partial mobility and movement, allowing me to turn my head a slight bit from left to right.

When they placed a metal halo on the top of my head, I could hear the sound of a crunchy cartridge as they slowly screwed it into place above each ear. Next, a five-pound bag was attached to ensure no movement as I lay immobile. I was placed onto a special bed where I could be rotated onto my front side and then onto my backside, a human rotisserie. I was provided a button to press when I could no longer bear the discomfort of lying flat on one side. When it became unbearable, I would send the distress signal. Two nurses would then come into the room, one at each end of the rotating bed, and count together…one, two, and on three, in unison, flip me over. The strain and pressure I felt in my neck just with the effect of gravity was excruciating, I dreaded every flip... but the relief of being re-positioned could not be overstated. Then repeat.

The only thing I could do on my own was drink from a straw and mostly sleep to pass the time. I could only be in two positions, front to back…back to front…ground hog day for seven long days. I received a phone call from my friend Liz. They placed the phone by my ear, and I remember telling her that I was "upside down," not sure if she knew what I meant, but I was looking down at the floor while I talked to her. One of the paramedics phoned me also, just to check in with me and see how I was doing. This was when I learned how they had found me at the crash scene…50 feet away from my car. Some key information, that I am really glad to know. Whoever this person was, I appreciated his kindness in giving me a call. First responders are some of the best people!

My parents came to visit me one time during my hospital stay. They were able to have Angie with them through all of this. She had just turned three years old, and my parents were always available. My bad behavior is difficult to re-visit as I write this. Looking back over my life, going out partying was the most destructive aspect and the most difficult to change. At the age of 19, this was just a bump in the road. Well, a very big bump, and many more would follow.

My entire length of stay at Sunnyside Kaiser was fourteen days, the exact same number of days that Angie had spent in Sunnyside hospital just a year and a half earlier. How often I have thought about this over my life, how close she came to dying that night with spinal Meningitis... then, for me to have nearly come to the same fate. I could have easily died in this crash, or I could have been paralyzed. These miracles have helped me to gaze upward in wonder. I know that I am no more special, but I have often thought of myself as having an Angel watching over me. I am so thankful for these blessings, to even ponder on how things could have been much different breaks my heart. If Angie had not made it, I don't believe I would have had it in me to make any steps forward. What would be the point? My entire "why" would have been gone. I was given a purpose, maybe by default or in a roundabout way, but I needed to make my way and had a responsibility to do so. This gift of becoming a mom set a foundation to move forward. I sincerely believe without this gift I would have continued to flounder, and the probability of worse disasters would have surely visited my life.

After completing the seven days of lying flat in traction, I was then wrapped into a full body cast, with my arms and legs unrestrained. This cast covered me from the top of my head down to my hip bones. I looked like a mummy with a full leg cast to boot. My face was exposed slightly, kind of like wearing a motor cycle helmet. The very top remained open, where my awesome roommate would pull my hair through and make a little pony tail. Both my arms were free, which allowed me to get a back scratcher through the openings. It was a massive hard shell that I would remain in for the next six months.

Before being discharged, two rehab nurses, one on each side of me helped me to stand up from the bed and take my first few steps. I had not stood up for about 12 days and could only walk a few feet as I re-learned how to hold my balance. As they increased, standing me up and taking steps, I bounced right back. After two or three days of getting myself back to independent mobility, I would be released.

I would return home to the little house I was renting with my roommate, LeeAnn. Very simple days followed, just her, me, and Angie all taking care of each other. LeeAnn was a CNA at the same Hospital that I was taken to the night of my crash. She was thoughtful and caring. I was so fortunate to have her as my roommate during my recovery. I had about three previous female roommates that I would advertise for in the Oregonian classifieds. I hated advertising for a roommate. I would place an ad in the share rentals section and just hope for someone decent. I wanted to afford living without needing a roommate, but financially, that was not possible. A good thing.

As I was lucky enough for her to answer my ad, under these new circumstances, she was just what I needed.

My night out had been to celebrate the end of my Fall term at Portland Community College. I was looking forward to all of my finals and was doing really well in school. I loved all of my classes and could not have chosen a better major for myself, though some classes became a little hard, such as third-term Accounting...but I was not trying to become a CPA. My Contract Law class was a sleeper. This could have been because it was my last class of the day. Other than that, I was well on my way...with my first year done and my GPA at 3.14, I was gaining ground. Now, in my 2nd year, my full intention to take my finals ended in disaster. Finals week came and went while I was in the Hospital. It was a tragedy after working so hard the entire term only to get my report card in the mail with an "I" after every class (incomplete). I wonder if my instructors wondered where I was. Maybe I should have found a way to reach out to PCC and explain my circumstances in order to take the finals through another method. All this was hindsight, of course.

A tiny silver lining was that I had disability insurance coverage with my U.S. Bank auto loan in the event I could not make my car payments. I purchased a used car in October, and was relieved to have had this coverage in place as the car was a complete "total" by December. It was a 4-speed… my first stick shift; at the time, I thought they were cooler and more fun to drive. Possibly all true, but certainly not in my favor being drunk.

By now, it was very close to Christmas, and my roommate and I rented a wheelchair…loaded me into her car, and drove to the Lloyd Center to Christmas shop. I should have felt differently I think, but it was all a little humorous. She was pushing me around the mall as I sat in the chair with my half-mummy body cast on and broken left leg fully stretched out, resting on the leg support. I'm sure I looked like a major crash victim (which I was) and probably got lots of stares. None of this mattered. It was time to resume life, and it was Christmas time!

My recovery was going well; the doctors at Kaiser were thrilled and actually somewhat surprised to see my progress and how quickly the break in my neck was mending. I could not have heard better news. The thought of having a fused neck? Thank God I did not have to suffer such a fate.

Breaking Free

I resumed Real Estate classes at Portland Real Estate School. This was another program offering all the needed requirements to take the RE exams. As I had screwed up College so badly, I opted to take the quick crash courses. I didn't want to lose ground; I couldn't tolerate the idea of letting this event ruin everything, get me off track, and take away what I had already started. I wanted to do whatever it took to stay on track with my courses. My dad would take me to night school in the evenings, a school on NE Broadway not far from their house, to finish up my Real Estate education. At that time, I gave up on the idea of finishing my 2nd year at PCC. I attended the entire course with my body cast on. I'm sure I looked ridiculous, but I did not care.

After six months of living in a strait jacket, my body cast was finally removed. My leg cast had been removed after the first couple of months, leaving a very large scar on my shin. I had a fairly good cut on my chin that was healing, and with the special ointment that they used in the Hospital, all of the abrasions on my forehead disappeared. I had fully recovered, the best part being I had full mobility of my neck. I could turn to the left and turn to the right. Everyone was happy.

This horrific accident, this self-induced screw-up for many, would have become a *turning point.* The thing one could point to that caused a total shift in behavior.

If only. It would take another 20 years to eliminate alcohol from my life.

CHAPTER SIX

Hitting Resume

It was 1980, less than a year since my crash when I met Mark at a party. This was my first boyfriend after Ray. Mark took the place of LeeAnn and moved in. Nothing much had changed. He was similar...a guy of my peers. We celebrated Angie's 4th Birthday. I would spend weeks planning her little parties, year after year. Her birthdays were hugely important to me. Each year, I tried to do different themes, a Care-Bear party, Chuck-e-Cheese, or Farrell's, where they brought a huge variety of ice-cream scoops covered with little plastic zoo animals. The employees would transport it as they zoomed around the long-decorated table, singing and blowing party favors.

Mark and I both got jobs at Yaw's Top Notch Restaurant. I was a hostess, and he was a server. We could work the same shifts and carpool. Yet, I would again get another DUI. I took off on my own to a bar on Sandy Blvd. He didn't want to go, but I didn't let that stop me. Coming home, braking at a red light, I slid the car into a telephone pole. Very scared, I turned the corner to park, hoping to flee home. Well, there was not enough time to get away. The cops pulled up and took me to the police station. They returned me home; Mark was very angry. I think things were much laxer at that time; as far as the DUI laws. I would get suspended and attend alcohol education classes. No, this was not getting my attention.

Mark moved to Palm Springs to make more money as a server, and I worked my way up with Yaw's from hostess to waitress. They started me out at a counter, where mostly single people would dine before I could serve tables. I quickly learned the ropes. Earning tip money clearly motivated my eagerness to advance and serve full tables. Yaw's was very popular in the old Hollywood neighborhood and famous for their burgers, French fries and gravy, and homemade pies.

In March of 1981, I passed the Real Estate Exams and was recruited by Tarbell Realty Co. I met with them to see about breaking into the field, and they mentioned holding open houses to meet potential buyers to get my feet wet. I knew that

I did not have the confidence to pull the trigger and actually join their real estate brokerage. Good thing. With interest rates hitting 18% and many brokers going out of business, it was an absolutely horrible time for all realtors. Shortly thereafter, Tarbell closed their doors. Many people expressed to me what it would take to break into this type of career; a rule of thumb, you would need approximately six months of income saved up to give it a go. That was a definite deal breaker. I knew that was an impossibility. Keeping a roof over my head was all I could do at the time. I was so young and immature…or maybe, more to the truth, I was still dabbling in the party life and felt compelled to keep this hidden. The whole thing made me feel so uncomfortable: stepping into the "normal" world and working alongside typical, healthy adults. The inadequacy I felt about myself was way too strong. It was not the right time.

The owner of Yaw's had a new vision for the restaurant, he did an extensive remodel… and added a cocktail lounge. This was a brand-new addition; I had just turned 21 years old and could now become a cocktail waitress. My best friend, Tammie, worked there and was able to train me. She was only a few months older and already had enough experience to teach me well. Mark returned from Palm Springs; he struggled with getting a good job. He eventually returned back to Palm Springs for good.

My parents spotted a very cute Duplex available for rent on the corner of 58th and Halsey. They also just lived down the street, so it would have been easy enough to notice the For-rent sign. I am so thankful that they happened upon this perfect little place for me and Angie to move into. The rent was $250 per month, and I was working full-time to afford it. We moved in on August 1, 1982, exactly five years to the date from my place on Fremont. It was a charming, classic, side-by-side, two-story duplex built in 1940 with hardwood floors throughout, Rose/Burgundy tile kitchen counters, and an unfinished basement for a washer and dryer. The ceilings had rolled corners and an arched wall leading into the dining room. I loved everything about it, all the charm of the era…not to mention the location. Normandale Elementary school was only two blocks away for Angie to begin Kindergarten.

I was able to work more flexible hours, taking a new job as a banquet waitress at the Red Lion at Lloyd Center. Most of the big banquets were on weekends, allowing me to begin manicuring school. From my first full set of Acrylic Nails, I continued to maintain them. Even after my crash, I went back to Nails on Broadway with my body cast on for my fills. The manicurists in the shop would have soap operas on while getting my nails done. I remember sitting there, just imagining how cool this was. What a great job... just sitting around, working on a craft project, and talking with people. That's how I viewed it, and I loved crafts. I was also very meticulous and detailed...very much a perfectionist. In March of 1983, I passed the Oregon board and received my manicuring license. I was hired at the first Salon I applied to, on 122^{nd,} and Halsey called Roman Holiday. Before manicuring school, I thought of going a more traditional route and spoke to the manager of a U.S. Bank about working as a bank teller. It was not a yes at that time, though he did call me back, offering me the job weeks later. I was surprised when I received his call and did not expect it. Wow, what an opportunity. To transition into a real job. I liked the idea of this normal job. It's what I truly wanted, but I knew myself. In the back of my mind, my proclivity to party was telling me clearly that I could not take a job like this. I wished that I could, but by now, I was thinking...*What if I partied the night before?* This job was serious, a real 9 to 5... so I declined.

The Salon that hired me was a hair salon where most of the clientele was older. The stylists were middle-aged and did a lot of shampoo/sets. They placed me right up front as you entered the reception area, with solid glass windows to the ceiling and a solid glass front door bringing in the beautiful natural daylight. Just perfect. There was a front receptionist handling the phones and large mirrors covering the walls, all the way down both sides of the long room, with swivel chairs spaced apart. The hair-dryer chairs had little stainless-steel ash trays in the arms, and my clients could smoke while I put on their acrylic nails. I also did back-breaking pedicures and regular manicures. I was paid on a split commission, and after paying the Salon a couple hundred dollars, I could keep 100% of my pay. After only a couple of months of being employed there, I was busy enough to quickly pay my monthly station rent and then receive the full amount of the services.

I began to meet many women who became regular clients. They would share great recipes, places to visit, and genuine friendship. Many of these women would stay with me for the next twenty years. I was planning Angie's 7th Birthday, and a nail client let me in on the perfect gift. It was a hand-crafted dolly bed, the large, oval woven basket was natural wicker, and the entire inside was padded and lined with pink and white checkered fabric with white ruffle finishes. I couldn't wait to give it to her!

In my limited capacity to truly *thrive* with my drinking style as a part of my life, my story was a mixed picture! As some success *would* come... fortunately; I also continued partying, mostly girl's night out, etc., though, mainly kept it to weekends. As a very young single mom, I would work hard, pay my bills, buy a new piece of furniture, make sure the house was spotless, put on my dancing clothes, and step out.

The dance floor was the highlight, the fog rising up off of the floor, a couple of strong drinks in me... it was play-time. The Salon was right next door to the Refectory, a busy dinner and Dance club that was very popular. It was always packed, and the dance floor called my name. Even the owner of the Salon stepped out onto the dance floor. She was a lot of fun and would do up my hair, full 1980s, with lots of hairspray.

Even though the owner was in charge of my pay, it was *almost* as though I was self-employed. I was able to set my own hours and days, which provided me with a lot of independence. I became fully self-employed when I relocated to "Tan your hide" in Downtown Portland on 4th and Alder, a salon full of tanning beds, another popular venue with round-the-clock clients. Here, I could rent my station, set my hours from 11 am to 7 pm, Tuesday through Saturday, and keep all of my own money. I loved being in charge of my own schedule. The full independence of working entirely for myself was absolutely perfect for me.

My dad and brother were wood-workers together and made me a solid oak manicuring table for my new job. I had a professional poster board made advertising a Special... full set of acrylic nails for $29.95. My books were full. I was one of the first few manicurists in the Portland area and got in on the ground floor. I was able to make my own way! The best part about all of this was that I didn't have to have a roommate. I worked full-time, breathing in those horrible toxic fume's day in and day out for the next two decades.

CHAPTER SEVEN

Next Abuser

When I was 23, history repeated itself. I suffered another four years of domestic violence under another horribly violent boyfriend. They say, "The faces change, yet the relationship remains the same." I've often tried to distinguish which one was worse, Ray or Craig. There was no answer; they were one and the same. The beatings were all alike, over and over again, and always alcohol-related. Neither of these woman beaters ever did it sober.

Instead of being 12 years older than I, as Ray was, Craig was a couple of years younger, but age made no difference. Both were carbon copy abusers. I honestly cannot recollect a legitimate reason that would cause these men to become so enraged and violently attack me. I was not a fighter nor an instigator, and I definitely did not have any anger issues. I think it might have been my passivity. It was not in my nature to stand up for myself.

There was no legitimate reason for any of this. I believe it was more of the same: someone expressing dominance and control over me through violence and fear. My low self-esteem undoubtedly contributed to it – that and my participation in the partying. Of course, I chose another drinker; I was doomed to repeat.

I did everything possible to keep hidden and conceal this other life…the dark events still plaguing me. Come morning, I would turn off the horror movie and block it out, pretending there was no there-there. I would apply make-up concealer where needed, wear appropriate clothing to cover my neck trauma marks, and just bury the pain and sadness. Again, I just accepted my circumstances. The abuse was kept from Angie as she would be at Grandma's and Grandpa's on the weekends. All would be a fuzzy blur. After heavy partying, the night would end, and only my bruises would remain.

My father had a small wood working business out of his garage with my brother called "Little Oak Shoppe." They made solid oak home accessories and sold them on weekends at the

Saturday market. He would bring Angie along on Saturday and Sunday to work the booth with him. I'm sure he loved having her along. She was adored by all the vendors. She was a beautiful and bright-eyed little girl. She was something very special, so kind and thoughtful.

My heart breaks as I recall where my life was at this time. I was involved with another awful person, someone who provided not an iota of true benefit to my life, and my partying was definitely not providing me with any benefit. Economically, there was the financial benefit to letting him move in, probably the biggest driver at the time. I wish so badly that I had been a better Mom. I wish I was not the way I was. If only it could have been different. Working five days a week only to spend my weekends drinking and getting beaten was incredibly pathetic. To endure this for so long says so much about me. I was so messed up and could not be sorrier.

My desire to have someone in my life caused me to settle. I chose the bad-boys...tall, dark, and handsome... though full of their own problems. I really don't get it. How could I go through this all over again? With Ray, abuse was all new to me, and I had no background to draw from. With Craig, I had a point of reference to draw from and realize that I allowed it, all for the relationship.

I would again hide all this abuse. I was a total doormat. I was hard-working, responsible, good with money, and had a home for them to settle into. I thought they would surely love me. I thought so little of myself I certainly did not demand anything more. You can also knock the shit out of me whenever you like. What kind of a signal does that send? How I felt about myself was the major contributing factor to choosing men like this.

The protecting them? The hiding of all of this was truly a big problem. The how and why I allowed it all to go on for so long is unexplainable. After another long night of abuse, I had to pull myself together to make it to a family reunion. I was a wreck, emotionally trying to shake off a beating and a hangover to boot. When I arrived at the park, I was caught off guard when my brother, Steve, asked, "Bren, what happened to your face?"

That set my heart racing. I knew my jaw line was all black and blue, and it did not go unnoticed. *Think quick! Say something*!

" Oh," I blurted out, "When I was opening up the cupboard, I accidentally smacked it into my jaw." I knew that sounded ridiculous, but I think it sufficed.

I have a separated shoulder from this relationship. I could have had surgery, but the choice was a big scar on top of my shoulder or a protruding bump. I chose the latter, which I still have today.

A peek into how sick this relationship was: The next day after a beating when he would see the bruises on me and ask if he had done this to me, I would tell him "Yes," and then I would actually want to comfort him while he expressed remorse. I was feeling sorry for him! I felt bad that he felt bad.

How twisted, how low did I need to go?

After these regular beatings, he would sometimes yell at me that he was just like his father. Other times, trying to justify the night before, he would angrily yell, "I'm a man, Brenda. I'm a man!" He also explained to me that while he was in these episodes of rage, all he could see "was white,"… whatever that meant.

Craig was also a cheater; I would find women's swimwear under the seat of his car after one of his late nights getting home. He had a Master Craft ski boat and called telling me some story of breaking down on the river, all to add cover to his infidelity. And then there was the time a summons was delivered to the door requiring him to show up to Court for soliciting a prostitute. The hurt I went through was a whole different form of abuse; it only made me feel smaller. It only made me feel less than. Somehow, there had to be something very wrong with me. Otherwise, why would he stray?

After getting home from work one evening, I once again suffered a new agony. He let me know that my strand of pearls and 14k gold chain was missing from my bedroom mirror. The pearls were real. I traded nail work for many, many months to work them off. He admitted that he'd picked this girl up on his way home from work, invited her in, and after taking a shower, he discovered that she had stolen my jewelry, and she was long gone. Unfortunately, it ended up that I was her victim, too.

The relationship finally ended when he said that he was going Christmas shopping with his best friend's Mom. He explained that she wanted him to help her pick something out for her son. He never came home. I lay awake all night, listening to every car on the street, waiting to hear him pull up and park. Morning came. It was over. After working the whole day without an hour of sleep, I went to stay with my parents until he moved out. When I stopped by the apartment to get some clothes, he grabbed me, wrapped his arms around me, and said, "Let's just get married."

I pulled away, finally realizing how unbelievably ridiculous this was.

I had a very strong friendship with his sister, Teresa. She came over often to dress up for girls' night out and style my hair. We were very close and often talked about how much we both wanted a good, healthy, normal relationship. We would talk on the phone for hours and joke and laugh that we would probably be a couple of old ladies in our rocking chairs, still single and alone. The friendship lasted years... until she was murdered. They never found her body, but me and the detectives knew without a doubt who did this to her... her ex-boyfriend.

CHAPTER EIGHT

Legal troubles

During my abusive relationship, my boyfriend would do the driving whenever we went out partying. That sure didn't hurt anything, considering my track record. Unfortunately, after our relationship ended, I became my own driver, which set me up for trouble. I was charged with a few more "driving under the influence" from the age of 26 to 28 years old.

On one occasion, driving down 122nd Ave after drinking with a girlfriend at her new home, I decided to go to my favorite night club on Halsey, the Refectory. After having a few drinks during the afternoon, I was feeling no pain, and I didn't tire. I just wanted to keep the party going. When I left my girlfriends, it was turning dark, and I was unaware of my faculties. I never had concerns about being impaired. Being intoxicated felt fine,

I guess. My brain was devoid of any apprehension as to whether I should drive or not. I just felt at ease and never experienced any alarm.

While driving down the highway, my headlights were not on, just my parking lights and I was busted again.

I was dropped back off at home by the police after being charged. Once again, I was in the fix-it seat. I had to get my car out of the tow yard. There was no way that I would be able to get a wink of sleep. I wanted to do anything I could to cover this DUI and make everything appear as normal as possible by morning. To deal with all of the fear and anxiety I was experiencing with every breath, I hitchhiked downtown at some ungodly hour to the police headquarters to get the information as to where my car was towed, then hitched another ride to the tow yard, paid for the tow and drove home.

To be honest, my life was so out of control. My DUIs would be at least two to three years apart, only to repeat…a recurring nightmare.

Again, rinse and repeat. I believed this popular bar had the police staking it out, watching for any potential suspects heading for their cars. I became an easy target, leaving the loud, hopping Portland club. When I got into my car and started it up, an officer quickly pulled up from behind me and blocked me in as I backed up. The police report said that I backed up into his bumper, though I cannot say that I remember this. Maybe it was noted in the report and did not happen, but I would have no proof, and it could have occurred as he pulled in so close. Well, regardless... another DUI.

I was now beginning to pay a much heavier price, i.e. (financially), as I needed some serious legal help from an attorney. I had retained him for my "driving with my headlights off" charge and now needed him again. My earlier DUIs were fairly straight forward, as I got away without having any representation, but things were changing, and driving impaired was becoming much more unacceptable. The MADD movement began in 1980, and was now very active and growing across the country. These offenses were becoming much more serious as they should.

The most difficult and biggest "cost" of any DUI was losing my driving privileges. There was no quick fix for this. My suspensions were for one year. In order to keep my life going, I would drive even though I was suspended. I guess you could almost say that I was living a double life and was covering up my *huge* issues. Not driving would be the tell-all! Exposing the enormous Elephant. Everyone would know of this Elephant...that would be way too difficult. There was no escaping *me*.

After each DUI, I would slow down the partying, get a girlfriend to drive...take a cab to the bar instead of my car, and count the months down until I was able to re-instate my license. My sentences were mostly paying fines, attending alcohol education groups, along with A.A. meetings. I was also ordered to attend a MADD Victim Impact panel and listen to each story of at least half a dozen women...all victims of losing someone by an impaired driver. The panel sat at the head of the room with photos of their lost loved ones placed upright in front of each of them. I should have tried harder to ponder on their grief. Admit to myself more than I was, that I was part of the problem. Instead of clinging to some false hope that, maybe, one day, I would get this all under control. I kept telling myself - and believing - that I was really not that bad. After all, I had not killed anyone.

During these periods I would follow through on everything that was asked of me in order to be in the clear of the Court. The "responsible" me. I took on and participated in every aspect of my sentencing... well, everything that I could... I could not give up driving. Most memorable was being sentenced to serve (so many) hours of community service. I could select how and where I wanted to serve my time, and I chose to complete my hours at a women's homeless shelter located in a fairly rundown part of downtown Portland's old town at the foot of the Burnside Bridge. My job description was to stand behind an old, ratty wood counter and hand out bars of soap and a towel to anyone wanting a shower. If the girl had clothing with her, she was able to trade her dirty items in for clean ones. I would turn around, and behind me was a wall of wood cubbies full of laundered clothes to hand them.

One afternoon, standing behind the counter…watching the clock to get out of there, I couldn't help to hear what sounded like a big celebration. A group of girls all gathered together, showing support for another gal who was pregnant. I guess they were having some kind of a baby shower. Kind of bittersweet, observing all of them so happy for the mother-to-be, regardless of being homeless. There was cake and balloons, and they were all having a great time. It was impossible for me to see this as a true celebration. The thought of being pregnant at that point in your life seemed terrifying to me. All of these gals seemed to be at such a low point in their lives. But, maybe in their world, this was not their reality. Best not to judge, though to me, it was rock-bottom, a low that I could not fathom.

I have to say, as many times as I went through it, the legal process *did* force me to take a *look* at my drinking. Still, I had my reservations as to having a *true* problem. I was not quite there. I would sit through many weeks of A.A. meetings. I would not have attended any on my own at this point, but I was required to. They weren't that bad; I did pay attention. I listened intently to all of the down-and-out stories, the damaged relationships and divorces, the loss of jobs and homes, taking them to the streets...literally. This was all so heavy and so extreme...how far down alcohol would take them? I was in awe and admired the part of their stories when they quit! When they fully eliminated all alcohol from their lives, that was so impressive.

How was that possible? How could they let go of alcohol? I was truly envious. Unfortunately for myself, the message that I believed or wanted to believe was, "Gosh, there is no way that I am like them. I just drink on weekends to socialize and have fun. I don't drink a fifth a day and hide the empty bottles around the house. I am basically doing OK."

I really didn't hear MY story...my story of a binge drinker. I sat through the meetings watching the clock, telling myself that I did not belong here. I just have to do my time. When comparing myself to the people in A.A., I saw a glaring contrast as to where I was in my life. I had a cute little duplex with nice things. I was making payments on a new car and working five days a week. The stories that I would hear week after week were not the story of me. This, of course, was problematic. So much of what I wanted to believe about myself, as far as how different I was from all of them, allowed me to continue. I had no intention of quitting drinking. To not be *fully* like them gave me a sense of hope. At least I wasn't where they were in life. I think I knew that I had a drinking problem, but I figured that I would just keep working on it.

As a young single-mother struggling with the continuous worry that I might never meet anyone worthwhile, get married, and have any semblance of a normal life, I held on to the only way I knew and continued with the old pattern of how to meet the potential one. I was absolutely dependent on the social lubricant. The thought of sober courting was an impossibility. I could never imagine meeting anyone and dating without alcohol. I guess it was all I knew. Alcohol accompanied me. I was way too uncomfortable without this magic elixir; my wiring was all messed up. Dating was the biggest reason I could not contemplate being alcohol-free.

It was a part of my life that just was; a part that I desperately hated, the dependence to cope, the not being a normal drinker. It was a huge worry. Fear of my future plagued me endlessly.

CHAPTER NINE

A Success Story

The paths of life! In spite of making so many wrong choices along the way… blessings can drop in, too. The hopes and dreams that never left my mind continued to forge me ahead. As I put out each of the fires that I had started, I did not lose sight of what I wanted more than anything else: SECURITY!

I was a renter. The first small house I was in I rented for five years. And now, I am also renting my adorable duplex apartment, close in, near my parents and mass transit that would also serve me well. I was an exceptional long-term renter and always paid the owners on time. I kept the place neat and tidy and maintained my yard, keeping the beds clear of any weeds. I hated weeds. Over the course of a couple of weeks, I became very ambitious and boxed up everything in my kitchen to prep and paint all of my cupboards, inside and out…and the drawer surfaces. Everything had to be sanded first to do it properly. Then, I bought all new hardware and waited about a week for the oil paint to cure before moving back in. I was definitely a little unusual in that regard, and I treated my apartment as my own.

As the years living there wore on, I was becoming more and more restless about being a renter. I started feeling that I was much more than renter material. I was beginning to feel over qualified, making someone else's place nicer…and it not being mine. I had a strong sense of what a waste it was to pay someone else for the roof over my head.

I had mentioned to my dad on multiple occasions my thoughts of wanting to buy some day. I just passed on my idea, my concept at the time, about buying my Duplex and having a renter on the other side to help pay the Mortgage. I'm not sure why I told him. I just wanted him to know what I was thinking. Why not? It couldn't hurt.

It was also very fun to mention the vision! I had no idea how I could actually qualify and get conventional lending with my manicuring income, but first things first. I had no clue if the owners would even consider selling. But if so, I wanted to be first in line. I needed to find out and finally asked them if they would ever be interested in selling one of the Duplex's. John and Agnus Skoog were both quite elderly by now, and I wanted them to know about my interests. Agnus's father had built the Duplex I lived in in the year 1946 and then, in 1948, built a like-duplex next door. After I spoke to them, they expressed that they were not interested and that they were all doing just fine as rentals. Well, that was that.

What do you know, about six months after I asked them about selling, Agnus got in touch with me. Somehow, I must have planted the seed as she said that they were willing to sell. The best part is that they were willing to sell on a contract, which took any concern about financing completely off the table. Not only were they offering to sell the Duplex that I lived in; they offered to sell the matching one next door. I could not contain my excitement; by now, I had been renting a total of 11 years and believed in my heart that I was more than rental material, and it was time.

At that point, I was only considering an opportunity to buy the Duplex that I lived in. Just that alone was a dream. I raced over to my dads to share the news that the owners had changed their mind and they would sell on a contract. I had no idea what he would say or what he would come up with. It turned out he was as eager as I was. We would become partners. Then he surprised me with, "Let's get both of them." Music to my ears. My grandmother had just passed away, and he had a little money. Such perfect timing for him to invest. So exciting, then; to make things more comfortable he said that he wanted to bring in Fred, a longtime friend and business partner. The purchase price was $120,000 for both, $20,000 down, and a contract for $100,000. We needed $7,000 each for the down payment, leaving $1,000 to open a checking account. My dad was willing to lend me $5,000 and I had the rest. He put it on a ledger, charged interest and I made small monthly payments back to him. He kept the books; I collected all the rent, cleaned the apartments, and screened new tenants. We teamed up on deferred maintenance, replaced windows and tiled tub surrounds, added a new professional landscape, and finished a couple of attic rooms. I consistently raised the rent and had a fondness for renting to single-mothers. It all worked out flawlessly, a perfect partnership.

My dad had a way with words. He said to me something that I will never forget. "Well, Bren, at least you will always have a place to live." That is so true and could not have been more comforting. He was right. It was the security that I had envisioned and why I wanted home ownership so much…not to mention that I was now going to cap my rent for life as property manager/owner. My new status is never to be a renter again.

After we closed, the owners wanted me to know that I was the only one that they wanted to sell to because of how well I kept up the yard. All their other units had tall weeds growing around the shrubbery and un-mowed lawns. My yard stood out to them and was instrumental in their decision to want to sell to me. I had no idea that one day, something I was doing would create my opportunity and fulfill what was only a dream. I believe that all of my hard work was blessed, possibly divinely, to change the seller's mind.

My dad had not invested in anything up to this point and only had social security income. As the years passed and rents increased, we all benefited with a little cash flow. Our partnership brought so much peace to my life. I really wanted a good life but, unfortunately, still wore a ball and chain.

CHAPTER TEN
An Agonizing Loss

It was a 4th of July holiday weekend, a beautiful sunny late afternoon that quickly turned into another one of my most traumatizing, self-induced nightmares. My younger brother called me and asked if I could get him and his friends a gram of coke. I'm immediately thinking this through. *I know, Bill. He is a cocaine dealer, and I could probably add about fifty bucks on for my trouble. Sure, no problem.*

I dated Bill's brother, Kevin, so I knew the house and where to go.

I phoned Bill at his house, and the phone was picked up on the first ring. The guy on the phone said, "Who's this?"

I replied that it was Brenda and asked for Bill and said I was wondering if I could come over to buy some cocaine.

He said Bill couldn't come to the phone, but the answer was yes, come on over. *Wow, that was easy.* I jumped into my brand-new car that I absolutely loved and had worked so hard for and headed right over. I had just received the free and clear title in the mail, as I had paid it off about six months early. *This is great, and I will be in and out. I will get Don his little party favor, which I figured he was eagerly waiting for, add on my little profit, and bring it right over to him.* I loved being able to make a little extra money. This was going to be a great weekend.

When I pulled up to the house, I was swarmed by Clackamas County Sheriff's vehicles. They were everywhere, surrounding the entire house. Bill had been busted. The person on the other end of the line when I called Bill's house was obviously a cop, and it turned out Bill was not even there. If I knew anything at all, which I did not, I should have made sure to speak directly to Bill. A major mistake only an unsuspecting idiot would make. I was out of my league, such an amateur, and so naive when it came to stuff like this.

Bill was a pretty big dealer in Portland and looked the part… wearing a full-length fur coat of some kind when he went out. I think it was leopard. He also planned on owning his own large "Cat" one day. He was so out there. He also dealt drugs out of a hotel room in the Red Lion at Jantzen Beach. He would stay there long term, he and his pregnant girlfriend. I learned from Kevin that she was a drug addict, and she and Bill would do coke all day and order room service while isolated at the hotel. The whole thought of this really bothered me. It was such a visual nightmare to think about being pregnant and doing coke. I had tried it several times and really didn't like it. Snorting the initial first line was really great; I loved the sharp, clear mind and fresh energy, but I would want to quickly tone it down with my favorite drug of choice… and chug down a few beers.

The officers quickly let me know that I was under arrest for "attempting to possess a controlled substance." As I had not had the opportunity to complete the transaction, it was deemed an attempt. I could not have been unluckier. There was no turning back. Drug laws had just been strengthened, and they would take my car. Such an extreme misfortune. I was caught up in the newest seizure laws, and I was screwed! I was placed into the backseat of the patrol car and taken to Clackamas County Jail to be processed.

Absolute fear and misery were setting in. *What the hell have I done? This is getting really serious; they just took my car…that*

I loved and had paid off early! I need my car. I need to drive; I need to work. I need help. What should I do? This can't be! I'm so scared and worried I cannot breathe. I'm terrified.

I was able to get hold of my youngest brother, Chris, for a ride out of the jail and then home.

This was a very long-suffering screw-up, and I never saw my car again! I contacted the only attorney that I knew, the one who had helped me with a couple of previous DUIs. We actually ended up dating a few times as he was freshly divorced; his wife had left him for his best friend. I think that was something that really devastated him, to lose his best friend *and* his wife. He took me skiing over for a weekend and had me over to dinner. None of this ever went anywhere. He was probably trying to move on, and neither of us were that interested in each other.

Since I had no idea what to do, I called him for some help. After explaining my newest trouble, he did mention that he was predominantly a divorce attorney (red flag) but he would help me. He asked for a $2500-dollar retainer, which, of course, I did not have. I had to take my horrible, embarrassing situation to my father and borrow the money. I could always make good on borrowing money as he could hold it back from our 4-plex cash flow.

As the weeks passed, I was not getting much information as to how things were going. Without hearing from him I felt very much in limbo. All I wanted to know was that he was going to be able to get my car back. When I asked him about this, he told me very clearly, "Don't worry until I tell you to worry."

Being told, "Don't worry," did pacify. At least he did not say, "That will be impossible." I hung on to hope.

The months rolled on, and I was back on the bus. I still commuted downtown, and on occasion, if the weather was bad, my dad would drive down and pick me up. I never asked him to come get me. It was such a treat when he did, as it was always dark, cold, and wet when I would get done working.

I remember talking to someone, telling them my situation, and they are telling me, "Brenda, you will get through this."

I was stunned to have someone tell me such an untruth. I had to get my car back. That was the only way that I would be OK, the only way that I would be able to get through this.

Holding on to some form of "hope" helped. It was just way too early to be so positive.

In hindsight, I probably needed a criminal attorney. I will never know. I do remember asking my attorney if it was time to worry yet. So far, he had never told me that it was. I often wondered *when* or *if* he was going to tell me that it was "time to worry." I was hanging on to his earlier words; trusting that he was in control and all would be OK. I really don't know if he did much of anything or if he could, for that matter. He did not charge me any additional fees for his services. I was really kept in the dark throughout the entire process.

Unfortunately, at the time my car was seized, the drug laws were against me. The fact that my car was paid off made it much easier to seize. I heard from someone that if your car is financed on installments, they would not want to have to make the payments to the bank. If I still had a large remaining balance owed…maybe, I could have held on to my car. It's possible they were making an example out of me. No matter what, it was a huge injustice. I was sentenced with an "attempt to purchase a controlled substance" but did no jail time. My car, however, was history, and the lawyer never told me "to worry."

Breaking Free

A big part of my life was attending a local gym. Early on I had joined the "Figure and Fitness Spa" for women on NE Broadway and went in the evenings to a Jane Fonda workout. Later, my new gym offered a stair master and aerobics. I was called the aerobic queen. I went in the mornings before work, and being short, I stood in the very front row. Losing my car definitely put a pause on getting myself to the gym. In spite of messing up my life...regularly, I got back to it. I found a junker car and pressed the resume button.

As my story has a heavy amount of gloom, much of it was bright. I was working at "Salon Nyla," a new downtown salon with several hair stylists. Here, I was upfront in the reception area again with tons of natural light. Nyla and I have become very good friends and are very close to this day. We've enjoyed several road trips, traveling to Crater Lake with Angie and her niece and a lengthier trip down the Oregon coast to the Redwoods.

Another perk from manicuring was my clientele. One of my long-term clients offered me her beach home to stay at. She owned a beautiful home in Seaside along the promenade, and I was able to trade her with nail services. She also hosted a "Princess House Party" for me. I was doing a few parties selling

Princess House products on the side to earn some extra money. Angie and I set it up together. I did my spiel about the products. She had so many people there I had a record number of sales that night. I was quite the envy at the next Princess House meeting. I think I earned about $300 dollars and boxes of Crystal.

I had befriended one of my tenants in the Duplex next door. She was a single mom with twin girls, and we could not have had more fun together. We were very much alike, single and a little wild. I would invite Nyla and all of them to come along on these all-girl weekends at this amazing oceanfront beach home. All the young girls could play together while we adults could drink beer. Shirlee was a little heavier drinker than I was.

A great guy she knew wanted to marry her, but she could not accept his proposal. He was pretty straight, and she had a little more partying to do. When her drinking got really out of control, she did an about-face. She got married and joined A.A. I was pretty shocked but completely understood. You know when it's time, and it has to be on your time. She did the right thing. I admired what she was able to do. She moved in with him, and our water skiing, partying at the beach, and campouts ended.

CHAPTER ELEVEN

Repeat Offender

I'm beginning to tire of recounting my DUI offenses. I have become my own worst enemy. Nothing has changed. I keep out of trouble for about two to three years, then bam. My next offense happened after being chosen to be the driver - the designated driver - as all of the people at the party were too intoxicated to drive. They wanted to go buy some coke, and I had no problem saying yes. I felt fine. Well, I always felt fine when it came to driving. I had no ability to know if I was over the limit. I did not have a gauge. I over-drank every time I drank.

So, here we go again... after driving the rowdy bunch to some apartment out in Gresham to make the deal, I remained in the car with a couple of others, waiting for the purchaser to make it back. When he returned, everyone was overly excited to get back to the party with their newly purchased party favors. The music was blaring, and I had a car full of people feeling no pain. I'm not sure if it was all the wild, animated activity taking place in my car in the wee hours of the morning that got me spotted by the police or if it was something that I had done wrong that got me pulled over.

It is all so pathetic, I know. While I was going through all of the DUI procedures, with everyone stuck in the car, I pleaded with the officer not to arrest me. I always tried my best to perform well on all of the tests for intoxication and thought that I might have a chance for some leniency.

It was a "No." I recall him saying, "Well, all of this is happening for a reason," somehow saying that this was for my own good. Somehow, I kind of believed what he was saying, but I just did not want to have to go through with it all over again for the umpteenth time. All the usual followed: suspension, alcohol group, and more AA meetings. Then, to reinstate my driving privileges, I would need to get a breathalyzer installed in my car.

The flaws in my life were glaring, but mostly to me. I had still continued to keep my drinking trouble hidden, for the most part. I did share with Angie this latest DUI trouble, but it was becoming difficult to keep up the façade. I felt horrible. I just wanted to come clean and be honest about what I was going through. An admission, a fessing up. I told her that I was going to clean this up and not drink. I would do better! All the legal trouble, in hindsight, would be stepping stones to getting alcohol out of my life once and for all. I wanted so much more out of life; I wanted a little more "normal."

I was envious to hear about what my *married* clients were up to. I enjoyed listening to them talk about building a new home or working on a major remodel. I would hear about their travel plans, even their long-term retirement goals. I pondered on this, "this" being married thing… something that should be so natural to one's life and yet felt so far off for me. The whole idea of coming to a point where you meet the one that you would actually want to get married to seemed remote. How did this happen? How did people do this? I knew deep down that I had the same wishes for myself. But the present day was still unfolding.

At the time, I was on an all-woman's Hood to Coast running team, attending night classes at PCC to finish up my Associate Degree and going to weekly counseling sessions. My good friend Nyla referred me to a woman counselor who lived in the very trendy Hawthorne neighborhood and worked out of her home. I started seeing her on a weekly basis. She lived in an old, vintage two-story home with a large wooden porch. She warmly greeted me at the door and led me upstairs to a bedroom filled with plants and simple furniture. The setting was very casual and comfortable. She was older, probably a true hippie in her day, wearing wire glasses and pulling her dark gray, wiry hair back into a ponytail. She wore a variety of thick, bulky socks and sat back relaxed, with her legs crossed and stretched out on the rattan coffee table. I sat directly across from her, where I could look out the window and see the tall leaf tree towering above.

As I briefed her during my first-hour appointment, I was somewhat perplexed when she gave me a confirming nod and a smile and told me, "I can help you, Brenda!"

"Really?" I'm thinking. The thought of this, someone I could confide in for the first time, someone who could truly examine me, was calming. I could not have been in a better place. She was offering a new client special at $25 dollars per visit for the first couple of months; and when the time came to pay full price at $80 dollars, she knew that I would have to drop

off from coming. She did not want this to happen. She wanted me to continue seeing her and graciously let me know that she was going to keep her fees the same. I was thrilled… and continued going weekly for the next two years. She hugged me at the door, leaving after each visit, and told me that she loved me. Each visit was the highlight of my week. I wanted help. I wanted to understand who I was. Well, the bulk of who I was, minus the alcohol. At that point, I figured that I had given her enough to start with to get a read on me. She also worked at a prison, counseling women who were incarcerated…just a step below where I was at that point in my life. Incarceration was looming for me as I *would* get into further DUI trouble.

For the most part, I wanted to get some insight and understanding of my repeated domestic violence and being beaten by men. This was where I had to start. This led to the bigger picture, where I began to share about my life with my bi-polar mother. I kept the drinking pretty much out of the picture, not that it wasn't a problem. I just could not expose it at that point in my life. I knew that I was not able to take that one on… at that time. First things first. I was there to deal with all of my previous issues in somewhat of a chronological order. I never wanted to get beaten again!

Breaking Free

I was ready and willing to rise above these bad choices in men. I no longer wanted to allow myself to be such a doormat. I was excited to get better and stronger, and truly enjoyed the hope of self-improvement by absorbing everything she said. Grey had to explain to me, and teach me what a healthy relationship looked like, how I was to be an EQUAL. It was a partnership. I was never to be less than a man. It was such a simple, clear concept. I just needed to be told. I would register every word in my brain; I needed to be re-programmed as to how I should be and how I should think.

I went out into the world without any expectations for myself. There were no guardrails in place warning me of any trouble, what to watch out for, and no real baseline to draw from making anything clear. Weekly counseling provided me with a new and necessary starting point. What I should look for and expect in a relationship was permeating in me, week after week. At the close of every session, walking to my car, I felt light on my feet with a big smile on my face. I felt renewed and hopeful. She was slowly transforming me, and I loved being re-shaped. She was injecting me with a new level of confidence and empowerment. My time with her was invaluable. She lifted me up, she gave me self-worth, she gave me value!

As I mentioned previously, I joined a running team. This addition to my life could not be understated. I was asked to join a group of a dozen girls to run the Hood to Coast relay. The starting line began at Timberline Lodge on Mt. Hood, with the finish line at Seaside, Oregon, on the coast. The team came together at the gym that I was going to regularly and took me from indoor aerobic classes to the open road. At first, I declined the offer to join the team and told the team captain recruiting people that I could not join because I was not a runner. Just as I said this, she pointed to another girl and said, "Neither is she." When I looked over at her, I immediately thought to myself, *if she can do it, surely I can do it too.* Knowing that she was not already a runner gave me all the confidence that I needed to join the team and accept the offer.

I started training the very next morning. I was committed. The first thing I did was go to a track near the gym to see how many laps I could do. I was spent at five miles, giving me my baseline. Most importantly, this first day out told me I hated the drudgery. I loathed going round and round the track, needing to count each loop. If that had to be my form of training, I would have had to reconsider saying yes and fully back out. I found the best way to increase my mileage was to train on the

205-bike path that had mile markers every quarter mile. As I ran along, I would seek out the next unknown marker ahead. This added a little more intrigue. The training was hard enough. Anything that improved the ability to stay with it was critical.

It was spring of '91, and by June, I was running competitively in many Portland races. This new sport was a great fit for me. I found that I enjoyed being outdoors, watching the miles go by, rather than an hour on the stair master or moving in place in an aerobics class. To meet me, I was just one of the girls, like all the other girls on my team (the normal ones). This was who I truly wanted to be. Being part of the team contributed to my well-being, adding to my confidence and making me tougher. For much of my life, the gym, the running team, and college classes were counter to a night out. It was a big contrast from being in charge of my day-to-day routines to losing control in a drinking setting. Several girls on my team and I took the Amtrak train to Seattle for a weekend getaway and a running race. I was the girl who suffered the hangover and had to suffer through the race that next morning. Mostly, out of total embarrassment about my overdrinking the night before and to add cover to my true misery, I never let on to how awful I felt. I would suck it up, put in some Visine, and change into my athlete hat. While we were all out partying the night before most of my friends would not have more than one or two drinks and nurse them while they hit the dance floor. I would cruise around the club so I could buy drinks on my own, away from everyone at the table. It was my way of not letting my gal friends witness my excessive nature, as I'm sure I would have two to three drinks to their one.

During the Summer of 1992, I resumed night classes at the PCC Sylvania campus. By this point, I was consciously trying to limit girls' nights out or going out with the hair stylists that I worked with in NW Portland. I was working in a small hair salon on 21st Ave with three stylists. I'm not sure if going out drinking was customary in this industry, but I worked with some regular partiers. Monte would pour straight booze on the rocks during his last client. I would give in from time to time, and we would all bar-hop together. I don't think any of us were moderate drinkers.

After a night out with the Salon crew, I noticed a part was missing from my bumper when I was leaving for work that morning. A flood of flash emotions came over me. *Where did I do this? How did I do this?* I had no recollection and wanted to deal with this immediately to fix and hide my screw-up.

Paging quickly through the phone book before I had to head off to work, I started calling junk yards. Luckily, I located the missing part and could have it replaced later that day. I breathed a huge sigh of relief and drove to work to start my day. Later, I left work to get the replacement part put on and quickly got back to the Salon. I felt relieved. The quicker I could clean up my messes the easier I could deal with the day. The story of my life: hit damage control. Carry on. INSANITY!

Well, all of this didn't go unnoticed. Monte said that he had seen that I had a damaged car when he arrived for work earlier that day and called me out for it. He wanted me to confess that what he saw was true.

I shook my head, saying, "No, I did not do anything to my car." Now that I had everything fixed, none of what he was accusing me of could be proven. I just denied such a thing and stuck to my story of complete contradiction. I knew he knew. He was insistent and took me to task, but as I was able to so quickly remedy the issue by getting my car repaired, we just had to drop it. The lengths I would go to save face!

Summer term Accounting ended and I registered for Writing 115 and Real Estate Finance in the fall of 1992. I could shorten my days at work and leave early for night classes.

Making my own schedule allowed me so much flexibility. I loved leaving work and hitting the I-5 freeway to PCC. Getting back to school was empowering and helped me feel a little bit better about myself. I struggled constantly with this dilemma of not being at a better place in life, basically harkening back to being my own worst enemy.

My day job (to be honest) was all service work, a decade of breathing in the worst smells of acrylic and airborne dust day in and day out. I enjoyed my clients, but it certainly didn't feel as though I was climbing the ladder in any way. I was just getting by, barely. I admired women who had business careers, especially a friend of mine who was a loan officer. Her nice clothes, pretty hair, and always arriving early AM to work were visions of success, and I was positive that she never had a hangover. The envy! I lived each day in quiet despair with how my life was going, and I knew that I was on a bad trajectory. To offset my alcohol abuse, I would do everything possible to add in good choices along the way, consistently seeking self-improvement in order to hold it all together and counterbalance my unshakable flaw. It was all an uphill battle. I was trying to outrun the elephant in the room! I knew that I did not have the power to take on the elephant. Maybe if I could just stay ahead of it, it would not take me out.

CHAPTER TWELVE

Drinking

The WHY or the HOW I became the drinker that I was, was really difficult to identify. There was no family history of alcoholism, and neither of my parents drank. No one drank at the annual family reunions, and my grandparents drank tea. There was never any alcohol in the home growing up, just the rare occasional beer my dad would have in the summer.

All I can gather from my non-alcoholic family background is that my relationship with alcohol came from a different place. There was something amiss. I was escaping. Everything that was emotionally wrong with me could explain why I would get locked into this dangerous pattern of drinking.

It certainly did not help someone who was emotionally damaged to have the worst examples out of the gate. My earliest memories of drinking beer were to get drunk. That is what I thought it was all about. I was only 12 years old when my best friend and I would sneak to the keg at her older brother's beach party. We weren't paid much attention, as it was very dark, in spite of the large bonfire burning several feet high. We filled the red plastic cups with fizzy beer and chugged it down as fast as we could to see how quickly we could get drunk, which resulted in my being doubled over and throwing up in the sand.

My introduction to alcohol was a party. I had not been around drinking of any kind previously. Therefore, I never witnessed any other style. As far as any social-drinking, I had not a clue as to what that was. The occasional single glass of wine with dinner or my dad having a beer after a long day swinging the hammer should have provided another drinking style or an example of how alcohol should be used. These parties taught me how you have fun and what the cool older kids did. I admired the older sister of my best friend. She was probably about 17 and had a boyfriend, was very pretty and fit, and wore very worn, faded-out 501 jeans with tears in the knees. I wanted my life to be like hers. This early influence would provide a smooth transition to future drinking. It was all thumbs up for me!

During middle school, some of the boys would shove quarts of beer down their pants from the small neighborhood market, and we would gather behind the school, passing them around. By freshman year in high school, I was going to Friday and Saturday night keggers every single weekend, and after enough practice, I would get past throwing up and could drink the night away. We were all beer drinkers, filling our red cups without limit. My peers never drank socially. I drank primarily with many older boys, and they all were on a mission to get drunk. I never once questioned it; I looked up to them. I wanted to be cool!

I also read a book about a girl's drunken childhood. It talks about a drink in your hand as an outward expression of pain. That drinking is a visible sign to the world that you're hurting. So heavy, so sad…this may have been me.

CHAPTER THIRTEEN

Love-Pain-God

This is the night that would change the entire course of my life! Unbeknownst to me, it was the beginning of my entire future. My co-worker, Vicki, at the Salon I worked at had a birthday coming up and had pre-marked my book, blocking out the evening hours of November 11, 1992, letting me know that I was not to book any clients. She was planning a night out, dinner basically; ha-ha…right! I knew better and had let her know that I was not wanting to go. I needed to refrain from going out with my early morning running and going to school etc. I would have to take a pass. She was adamant and was not going to allow me to get out of it. It was her Birthday, and I knew that I was never going to hear the end of it. I felt if I did not go, I was sending a message of some sort, possibly disrupting our Salon unity and I didn't want them upset with me. But truth be told…deep down inside, the real reason that I wanted off the hook was that every night out ended up the same. We all partied way too hard!

The evening started as planned, and we all went out to dinner at a fairly nice restaurant in NW Portland. During the entire dinner, the rounds of drinks kept coming, and the party was on. We were all primed and ready to continue celebrating. This was exactly what I was afraid of. After leaving the restaurant, each with our own transportation, we met back up at our next stop. Now, keeping it more casual, we went to a pool hall called the Gypsy, located on the trendy NW 23rd Ave. We all filed in and bellied up to the bar, ordered drinks, and let the booze keep the party going. By now, the room was loud, and our so-called dinner night out was rapidly transforming into typical bar hopping. None of the evening was about small talk or, for that matter, Vickie's Birthday. We were all just co-workers and basically, none of us was paying any attention to one another. We all had different agendas, personalities, and interests. For me, I was single, and my trusty social lubricant was in full effect. Now, it was time to place a quarter on the pool table. By now, Scott, Monte, and Vicky were cutting loose in their own way and the rest of my night took on a life of its own.

I was back at the bar and not paying attention to the pool table when the most handsome guy came up to me to let me know that I was up. It was my turn to put the quarter in. He had a friendliness about him, a warm smile, and deep blue eyes that pulled me in. We were a couple of magnets that collided in the night to the point where I completely blew off my co-workers and was captivated. We left the Gypsy together and went downtown to another nightclub to go dancing. He left his friend behind, and we went in my car. He drove. The club we went to had a live band, and it was close to closing time, just enough time to get onto the dance floor to finish the night when we started kissing. I truly was swept off my feet. His charm, good looks, and the fun we were having together made the blurry, intoxicated night magical. My memory is not the clearest, though I did go to his apartment. Not a surprise.

The next morning, when he walked me out to my car, he asked me for my phone number. I wrote down my number and handed it to him. and just wanted to get myself home as quickly as possible. Thankfully, as I looked around at where I was... I was less than a mile from my house. His apartment was one main street over from mine. Now that I was all sobered up, I cared less if he ever called me or not. I was way too upset with myself, the exact reason that I was not to go out drinking. I let him know that I had a daughter at home and how bad I felt that I was not at home. I wanted so much to do better, to be better, and there I went again.

As I started my car, he said the kindest words. He said that a bad mother goes out and doesn't care and that a good mother cares. I appreciated those words. I felt thankful that he did not see me as a girl-of-the-night loser.

When he called a couple of days later, my daughter answered. I guess they talked for a few minutes, and he let her know that he wanted to ask me out. When I came to the phone and settled into sober conversation, I began to get to know him for the first time, you could say. The whirlwind night had come to pass, and I really had no interest in anything further. Mostly, based on where we met, as I had met most guys in bars, I had my guard up and didn't want anything to do with a partier...that much I knew. Basically, done that, did that, and figured that nothing was going to be different here. Honestly, I did not know a thing about him...or if I did, I surely did not remember and let him know that I was not interested in going out and that I wanted to stay out of bars. As we talked, I slowly was realizing that all of my pre-judgments were wrong about him. I learned that he was a college graduate and had a great job in health care. I have to say, I think hearing this caused a 180 in my thinking. As we talked for a while, I was able to reassess my biggest concern that he was not a barfly. I ended up having a completely different take on who this person really was, and we set up another date.

When he arrived at my duplex apartment, my daughter opened the door. As I came into the living room, she ducked herself behind the door and mouthed the words "He's cute" with a big smile on her face. I was so relieved. That touched my heart. I really did not know what she thought, but her comment about him eased my worries, and I felt that she approved. Going out together was very casual and comfortable, and things took off. We began seeing each other regularly, and I was back in the whirlwind.

When Thanksgiving arrived, he sent me a beautiful dozen red roses. In December, he had personalized Christmas ornaments made not just for me but for Angie, too. He took us to his parents for Christmas. Both Angie and I were welcomed with open arms. In January we were skiing at Mt. Bachelor. Still, part of this amazing new relationship included alcohol, such a common aspect at the time. So much of our life had its similarities. As we grew closer over the next several months, I could not believe how much we had in common, and I was definitely falling in love. He came along on a weekend getaway with my family to the coast, where my dad had rented a beach house, and then took Angie and me to Disneyland.

Possibly because I was five years older than Bob, or who knows…I guess I was a little ahead of him in where *I* was in the relationship and what I started hoping for. I had never come close to meeting anyone that I would want to marry. Come to think of it, I had never been in love before. I started having aspirations for a future together and was hoping that he might be on the same page. As the months passed, then a year; I was making it known where I wanted things to go. I didn't want to waste my time with someone who would not want the same. I thought of the four years that I had wasted in my last relationship that was going nowhere and was never going to go anywhere. With the two years of counseling under my belt, I was more prepared to go after what I wanted and let go of a situation that had no sign of going anywhere. I was now thirty-three and was starting to make, trying to make better decisions.

As hard as it was, I made that decision. Without some kind of promise from him that we were on the same page or heading toward a future together, I broke it off. I could see no benefit in continuing the relationship. I wanted to go into protection mode (for myself). Something as serious as marriage could not be pushed on someone. It had to be one's own decision, and it was not the time.

I suffered greatly with our blissful romance ending, and gave it my all to stay strong. My income was going down at the Salon I was at. So many people were getting into manicuring services that I took a part-time job at my brother's company to run the embroidery machines a couple of days per week. We also partnered up on a ratty fixer-upper just across the street from my 4-plex. It was in such bad shape the seller offered it to us on a contract as it could not qualify for any conventional lending. The sales price was $50,000. This was another great decision and project to get me through the breakup. Together, my brother and even my sister-in-law and I transformed this little house, and I became the property manager.

I re-located my manicuring services to a much more professional, busy salon in John's Landing where I could keep my books full with so much more clientele. Definitely another better decision for myself, along with my running focus and night classes. I endured.

I found the biggest *relief* from all the pain of my breakup was when I accepted Christ. I needed something big, and this was it. After months of anguish, I found myself at an unbearable low. After much reflection and courage to accept this truth, I started realizing how the horizontal world can scorn, bringing hurt and pain. I was living in that world, the horizontal, and not doing a very good job of it. I was living and leading my life on my terms and started accepting that maybe I didn't have everything under control. This new thinking was really starting to make sense. It was so glaring and obvious. If everything I was doing was right, how could I be suffering this much? Maybe my way was not *the* way? I had not wrestled with this battle of "me" versus "something bigger" ever before. I wanted what I wanted! And I wanted Bob to marry me. Well...I wasn't making that happen. I surrendered my life and put Jesus first. I did not want to be in charge anymore. I wanted Jesus to be in charge... and it was this decision that brought me immediate peace. I belonged to Him.

My introduction thus far to God was through St. Mark's Lutheran Church, which my mom had us attend regularly. She piled my two brothers and me into the old white station wagon with a dark red interior to go to Sunday school, which I never looked forward to. I had trouble with car sickness and would become nauseated and throw up every Sunday on our way, not a good start to wanting Church. On top of that, I did not enjoy my time there, sitting on cold metal chairs along wood banquet tables. We were partitioned off into different groups by our ages, separated by plastic panels that could be pulled into place. Our lessons were held in the basement of the Church, where you were surrounded by concrete. There were a few tiny windows atop the concrete walls to bring a little filtered light in, and the floors were smoother, polished cement, which added a coldness. On occasions, say Easter, we could all go upstairs to the big Church. This would be the one day of the year that my dad would attend, and we all took a pew together as a family. These experiences did not speak to me either. I think the hymnals and the singing were what I disliked the most. My mother had mentioned my whole life that she could not sing or carry a tune to save her life, and somehow, along the way, this became instilled in me as well. Maybe she told me that I would never be able to sing. I definitely could see this as highly probable. I cannot think of an encouraging word ever spoken by her. The thought of singing in church was dreadful.

By 8th grade, you went through Confirmation. Part of this ceremony was to meet with the Pastor beforehand, one on one, to let him know why you wanted to be part of the big church. That was the next step, a rite of passage, I guess. I had no answer. I sat there trying to think quickly about what I should say or what I thought he wanted to hear. I thought as though it was a test that I had to pass, and I was so uncomfortable trying to say the right thing to please him. I just fumbled through it. Hopefully, a little mustard seed had been placed in me, and I am thankful that my mom made the effort she did to introduce us to God. I would just have to meet him at another time.

Bob and I talked about his faith; he had become a Christian late in high school. I learned how important this was to him and how the people that he had met during this time were instrumental in much of the good that he created for himself. During our wild ride of a relationship, we were both still misbehaving, which I know caused some of the conflict. I know he wanted to do better, too, and get right with God. Breaking things off was the right thing to do for both of us.

I was intrigued enough by his faith that I wanted to understand all of this more. What did I have to lose? It wasn't as though I was thriving with *my* hands on the wheel. So, I started dabbling. I began attending several different churches to find out if any of this was for me. I started tuning in to Christian radio and even started watching TBN. I wanted to know what this was all about. I was so curious - this whole Christian thing? I knew the traditional churches were a no-go for me, and after attending a "unity" service, I quickly learned the churches that never uttered the word "Jesus" and only "Great Spirit" were a no-go as well.

I found my fit after attending a non-denominational contemporary Christian church out in Troutdale. The Church was fairly new, called Riverside Community, and they used the auditorium at Mt. Hood Community College. I was in disbelief about what I had stumbled upon or was *led* to. No more hymnals and high-pitched singing; no more white-haired buns and pews of elderly people. This was such a contrast to anything else that I had been to. I went weekly and soaked it all in. The live music was so much more spirited, with electric guitars, drums, and lyrics displayed on large screens that brought you to your feet. Most surprising was the casual dress.

The guys in the band had long hair and wore jeans and flannel shirts. This was so cool. The whole theme was "just Jesus!" I knew that it didn't need to be anything more than that. Simple and pure.

As I drove each week to the campus, I had time to listen to a minister on the radio, probably a good 45-minute drive to my new Church. Each Sunday, he closed with the sinner's prayer. It was this prayer asking God to come into your heart and be the Lord of your life. It is a point of faith where you become a believer and put your trust in a higher power. I listened each week to this prayer, each week stopping short of accepting this free gift. I was held back by my lack of worthiness. I did not think that I was at all good enough. I had this idea that I could not be accepted until I changed my life. I knew that I partied, even though I was finding ways to limit it. There was no way this lifestyle was going to fly with God. As I listened to the message, week after week for nearly six months, I started hearing something different. The message was, "Just come," just come as you are. It was no longer what I had thought previously that I was not worthy. My coming to faith derived from a spirit of acceptance and trusting God's love for me, that I WAS good enough, that I was worthy in his eyes. I believed him to be a forgiving God and that anyone could enter at any point in their life. He knew everything about me. He knew my struggles and my shortcomings. That was the whole point - "just come," come as you are. He was calling me, Christ at the door, knocking. To my surprise, one Sunday, on my way to Church, I made it through the entire prayer. There was nothing holding me back, and I broke into tears. I was born again! So simple, yet so difficult. I never looked back. I will remember that exact moment forever. I think one of the first things that I became most aware of after that was that I had a place to give thanks. I started feeling more gratitude. I was thankful for what I did have. I loved my new Vertical relationship.

Even though I was making strides in the right direction, trouble had not fully ended for me. The owner of the newer Salon that I joined put on a get-together across the street at a Mexican cantina for all of us girls. It was the spring of '95. After my fill of Margaritas, driving home through a windy four-way stop, an officer lit me up. The cop was just sitting there at a convenience store and noticed something that I did. I was arrested and taken to jail. I arranged for someone I knew to come to pick me up from jail the next morning and take me to where my car was towed so I could get back home. I called in sick at work. I had never called in before, though, under the circumstances, this was way too difficult a day to pull off work. What was going to happen to me legally took months to reveal itself. I knew it was jail!

I continued working hard at the Salon, as well as the remodel that my brother and I had ventured into. I was still brokenhearted that Bob and I were not together anymore and occasionally slipped in a quick little prayer to let God know that if it could still ever be, I still wanted it to be Bob. Then I'd look up and say, "Just so you know."

It was a little silly, and I got a little chuckle out of it. I enjoyed letting God know, just in case. I thought it couldn't hurt. For the most part I gave it all over to God and fully accepted whatever was to be; I did wonder, though, what my life was going to look like. Was I going to just get old and forever be single? I could not worry about such things. Believe it or not, I had a strength in me that pulled me through each day. I knew that there was nothing that I could do. I had to let it all go and trust God that he had my life in his hands. The freedom to give my burdens over took the weight off. I could no longer carry them.

Then!!!

This is my entry in my journal, just as I had written it:

7/14/95

Dear Heavenly Father,

To the Lord of my life, I must say…I do believe in miracles. Dear Lord, thank you so much for mine.

You won't believe it, but since I last wrote, all things are new. Finally, the love of my life has asked me to marry him!

7/17/95: Received formal proposal this evening and a beautiful rose and prayer.

So much to go on and on about. It doesn't seem real yet. I will tell my parents tomorrow. I am so very, very happy!

Thank you, Bob!

I love you so much.

CHAPTER FOURTEEN

The Party's Over

Bob and I married 16 days after he proposed. We dovetailed in on a family reunion that was held every year at Laurelhurst Park. It was a beautiful sunny day in July, only two days after my 35th Birthday. His parents and brother showed up, and with my daughter by my side and immediate family all in place, I needed nothing more. Maybe hearing all the harsh rhetoric from my mom about ever wanting a big wedding shaped my thinking. Who's to say? I actually never put any thought into it. I had never envisioned such a day. My sister-in-law provided the most beautiful cake decorated with fresh flowers, and my brother took all the amazing photos.

The fall after we were married, I was sentenced and served two weeks in Multnomah County jail for the DUI charge from the previous spring. Yes, the real deal: full incarceration…and time to really start paying for my behavior. I was able to keep this unbelievably embarrassing circumstance from getting out to any of my co-workers or clients at the Salon by saying that I would be on a two-week vacation and then could resume work. Immediately after my jail stay, I was transferred to a work release program for another couple of weeks, where you could leave during the day. This allowed me to continue to work full-time, though I had to check back in every night until I could be released again the following morning.

I can't be thankful enough for getting married. It was almost as though I had a knight in shining armor to take me to work each day and drop me back off at the facility every evening. For better or worse, I guess, we definitely knew that both of us were far from perfect and just loved and supported each other in spite of our shortcomings.

I was released just days before Christmas. It was such a relief not to spend my nights in lockdown…and not spend my first married Christmas in a women's dorm. My mother was having another bipolar breakdown at this time, so I was able to host Christmas. I had all of my family over, including my mom.

She was still in the manic phase somewhat and had not been admitted for care yet. In spite of decades of criticism from her, I did not dwell on this or condemn her in any way. Christmas was my turn; I loved the decorating, planning and preparing food and cherished having Angie help me.

I absolutely loved my new life. We started setting a goal to buy a house, and I started a savings account. We were living together at the duplex but wanted to move up. Just a block and a half down the street, an elderly woman had had her house on the market, and it had not sold. She was offering contract terms for the cutest little house, and luckily for us, it was still available. It was neat as a pin and move-in ready. When we showed up and told her we wanted to buy her house, we couldn't miss her little shoes sitting by the door, and we could see that she did not wear shoes inside. After closing the deal and getting the house, we started slipping our shoes off in the mud room before entering. Her name was Treny. Treny started the no-shoes trend.

By now, so much was going right. It was the American dream... except for the elephant in the room. We both enjoyed those nights out after a long week of work, but a Saturday night out led to a dreadful Sunday. I loved being fresh in the mornings and getting my jog in, but about once a week was Groundhog Day. Maybe for many, this would be acceptable. I actually thought it was for the longest time. It was well deserved. After working a long week, I looked forward to it, kind of like the "Calgon, take me away" commercial.

I began to feel a real setback each week as I nursed a hangover. Now that I was in my mid-thirties, they lasted longer. I would feel so awful and tired, along with a horrible headache. The pattern was really getting to me, and I started talking to God about it. After a night out, I would head out on a short little jog in my neighborhood to shake off the poison, and I started apologizing to God about this merry-go-round of behavior. I truly, deep down inside, wanted it to end, but I knew that that would not be possible. I saw it as a condition that I had, like diabetes or high blood pressure. It was part of me, and I had to accept it. I wanted God to know how very sorry I was and took full responsibility. I wasn't asking him to take this burden from me. That was way *too* big of a prayer. I concluded that that would be impossible. I could never see that this affliction could or would ever go away. I just wanted him to know that it was what it was, and I was just going to submit to it in total defeat. I was admitting to God the impossible.

As I can't say this with absolute certainty or knowledge, I do believe that my path was altered in a divine way. One will never know, but this life-changing event came so suddenly. After my prayers of apology and defeat and personal surrender to what I knew would or could never change, things would be changed by a miracle. As I look at this now, many years later, I believe it to be the final straw… a gift, a prayer answered.

The night that changed everything, I drove us home from a pub about a mile away from our home and was blinded by the brightest lights I'd ever seen as I pulled into the driveway. It was the police (again) pulling in behind me. I was arrested for driving under the influence.

Little did I realize at the time that this would be MY TICKET TO FREEDOM!

CHAPTER FIFTEEN

A Full Surrender

All of this was my own doing. I insisted on driving, as usual. I felt fine and took the wheel. According to the officer, I was driving without our headlights on. All of this needed to happen. I needed to be stopped, literally!

This next journey of my life was a long time coming, and I made it! With the help of my loving and supportive husband and a very scary judge, I am now completely sober and alcohol-free. Actually, I should probably credit the grace of God first. This entire, most amazing transformation can only have occurred with some kind of superpower, a power greater than myself, my Holy Spirit.

Getting sober requires a team of support. What I had gone through was the only way. A strict judge put me in jail again, for a few days anyway, before I was hooked up to an ankle monitor. I could only leave home for work during specific hours and days, then had to return home immediately. And while back at home, at any waking hour, an alarm would sound, causing me to race to the blaring machine to shove the clear plastic tube into my mouth and blow into a breathalyzer. All this equipment was brought in and set up at home, and I was required to take random lie detector tests, answering questions regarding any drinking or driving, along with regular one-on-one visits with the judge, an older woman, very stern and strict, giving me my much-needed shaking up.

This extreme legal trouble was the catalyst for my entire success story. It was critical. This was by no means an easy journey. For the life of me, I am baffled at how extremely difficult it has been. To finally get to this chapter...after 25 years! It was as though I was teetering on a mountain top, a mountain top of choice. The decision was mine, all mine, and mine alone. Life has now gotten you to this place, a place where you could really see clearly. How much more clearly do you need to see? I mean, REALLY! What the hell more do you need? YOU CANNOT DRINK!!!!

This dreadful reality was before me: saying *goodbye* (once and for all) to my biggest comfort and security blanket, completely letting go of the trusty, reliable drink that could take all of my cares away.

The flip side was that I had an opportunity for a new reality, and I needed to grab this blessing with all of my might. How are you going to play it? What are you going to do? Your usual, your... try to fix it, hide it away, and resume? Fortunately, this was a pathetic thought and would not be my decision. PRAISE THE LORD!

I experienced bouts of fear, even mild panic at times about whether or not I could really do this. I had no idea, but that didn't matter. That was not to be my focus. What mattered was doing everything possible to help me get to where I wanted to be. To only focus on the enormous elephant in the room and nothing more, to support and assist me in what I truly wanted. Now was the time. Now was my chance.

I admitted myself to outpatient treatment at Providence Health and joined a women's group that met twice per week. I had a counselor and completed all the assigned material. I also joined an AA group that met every Saturday located in the Providence Hospital. With Bob's full support, he found a group that we went to together, a Christian 12-step group called "Alcoholics Victorious." I jumped in with both feet. It was *now* or *never*. The hope and possibility of getting alcohol out of my life was *bigger* than trying to find a way back to my old friend.

I grew stronger, one step at a time. It was working, and the prize was for the taking. The want of change was genuine. The vision, the freedom from cops and judges, could not be more exciting.

Here is the actual quote I wrote on August 26, 1999, two months after my ticket. *"Today, I am ready. It is time to accept the things I cannot change. I pray daily for God to heal me. I look forward to my meetings. I enjoy going to my groups. I am going to stick it out. This is what I want. I want recovery - all of it. I am so thankful for my past sixty days. I have not wanted to come near a drink. I want to be successful. I want alcohol to be gone forever."*

Month after month, I stayed on course. Then, year after year!

Alcohol/substance abuse is such a personal challenge. The elevator is going down and you can get off at any floor. Many get off early; the most difficult to ponder is how many take it all the way to the bottom, not ever stepping off. I am so grateful that I was able to get off this going down elevator. Going down any farther would not be of any benefit. I did not need a lower floor. It had my attention.

This affliction had contributed to more than 25 years of heartache, legal trouble, danger, worry, hopelessness, and shame.

Today, life without alcohol allows me to live my best life. I am an early bird; I crave jogging for miles and hiking to mountain tops just to stand and take in all the beauty around me in *gratitude*.

I will experience everything SOBER. I will live life on life's terms. I can live each day being me, in full charge, completely free from the force of alcohol and the consistent pull it had toward the next drink. It is a *freedom* that I had never before known. I will miss nothing, no longer wracking my brain, trying to remember the previous night's events. There is such peace in knowing that I no longer have to alter myself.

Keeping alcohol in my life was bondage, a type of force that was stronger than I was. It won out for way too long. Sobriety allows me to think and feel much deeper. My gratitude for life and continued self-improvement fills the day.

I am no longer afraid of the police on the road as they pull up behind me. My heart no longer skips a beat, pounding with fear that my license is suspended or that I'm driving without insurance! All of that I went through during my drinking years.

I believe the biggest, key piece to winning the battle to sobriety was the help of God. It does not matter at what point you trust in him, though part of the process is to give your life over to the care of God. This is what allows the transformation, the work being done within you that you cannot see. Most surprising has been the complete removal of any desire to drink, as though it was plucked right out of me.

This pathway to Christ began with my now husband. How different the life I have now would have been without our colliding in the night! I suppose this could be a book in itself. The despair I was in after we broke up led me to the Lord, full stop! A necessary development; for all things to be added unto you. God first!

Now I live in total gratitude, never to say there are not difficult days but I chose to start there. First, in gratitude, then prayer. Life is still going to happen, and I need God with me.

I'm living proof that all of the emotional damage, domestic abuse, and self-f-ups do not have to dictate your future. My life has not hardened my heart, only strengthened it!

THE ROAD - The wrong road? Or the road I was meant to take?

That's one of the biggest questions I ponder, as I have always heard that everything happens for a reason. Does this mean that this is exactly the life that I was supposed to have? That's a tough one. I really don't believe that's the case. I do believe it's best not to have to go down such difficult roads, but I also think it's important not to be overly protected. There has to be a happy medium. I guess the right balance would be ideal. It can get so confusing because experiences, even extreme hardship, can add teachable moments to one's life. Therefore, hardship serves a purpose so long as you learn from it and make the necessary changes and corrections along the way. Otherwise, it is all for nothing. That's the rub!! The ultimate Mystery, the ultimate CHALLENGE!

The journey to FREEDOM, freedom from being abused, from dependence on drugs or alcohol, can be a difficult one but is life changing. Wear ever you find yourself in your own struggle, if you're hurting or feel hopeless...escaping will never make anything better. If you are on this journey of change. I wish you heart felt success.

Don't stop. Don't give up. Keep dreaming!

Breaking Free

Brenda L Gauper

ABOUT THE AUTHOR

Brenda is currently living in Portland, OR. though spends a great deal of time in the Southwest. She is happily married to her husband of 29 years. Her grown daughter is also happily married with three children. Currently she spends her time doing property management, her love of Real Estate and investing has led way to early semi-retirement. The flexibility allows time for travel, jogging and hiking. She also has a love of photography and preparing great heathy meals.

Her days are very simple, spending time with close family and friends...but most of all, with her husband. She loves getting up early...before sunrise to enjoy the first light.

Her story, or her ability to tell her story came as a strong inspiration hit her while out on a jog and she could not get home fast enough to start writing. It was July 27, 2022, just one day before her 62nd Birthday. After writing the first chapter, which was the entire motivation at the time, she decided to tell it all. The good, the bad and the ugly. Her current hopes and desires are for her story to touch the women and girls still suffering from domestic violence, alcohol/substance abuse or any other form of abuse that brings only suffering.

Breaking Free

May you Break free and be made whole!